Welcome to *Be Your Best*

I believe that there are different areas of our lives in which we all regularly need to begin again. It's in these places we need to draw a line separating us from what we've known in the past and move forward with a new outlook based upon the truth of God's Word.

In order to make a fresh start, we need to be willing to let go of what lies behind and take hold of what lies ahead. I believe this includes getting a fresh start regarding how we see ourselves, the way we think God sees us, and what we see before us in our future. As we begin to see ourselves the way God sees us and get a good picture of the things He desires to bring about in and through our lives, our outlook on life can take on a whole new perspective.

God has a good plan for each of our lives. He says, "For I know the thoughts and plans that I have for you, says the Lord, thoughts and plans for welfare and peace and not for evil, to give you hope in your final outcome" (Jeremiah 29:11). In order for us to see this promise become a reality, we must choose to look away from the past and look forward to what God has ahead. He tells us, "Do not [earnestly] remember the former things; neither consider the things of old. Behold, I am doing a new thing!" (Isaiah 43:18–19).

Being your best involves getting a fresh view at how you see yourself. God wants to do something new in you *right now*! He wants you to be your very best in life—to fully be the person He created you to be. The possibilities are unlimited. It doesn't matter how young, old, rich, poor, educated, or uneducated you are or even how many weaknesses you have. God can even make miracles out of your messes!

Every day God gives you the opportunity of a *fresh start* with a clean slate—in every area of your life. Open your heart and ask the Holy Spirit to point out areas of your life where He wants to give you a fresh start. In Him there are no dead ends—only places for new beginnings!

Believing His best for you,

Joyce

CONTENTS

PERSONAL GROWTH

HEALTH

PRIORITIES

SPIRITUAL MATURITY

FINANCES & SUCCESS

CONTENTS

106

113

84

Be Your Best
JOYCE MEYER

All Scripture quotations, unless otherwise indicated, are taken from the *Amplified® Bible*, Copyright © 1954, 1958, 1962, 1964, 1965, 1987 by The Lockman Foundation. Used by permission. www.Lockman.org

Scriptures noted NIV are taken from the *Holy Bible, New International Version®*. NIV®. Copyright © 1973, 1978, 1984 by International Bible Society. Used by permission of Zondervan Publishing House. All rights reserved.

Scriptures noted NKJV are taken from the *New King James Version*. Copyright ©1979, 1980, 1982 by Thomas Nelson, Inc., Publishers.

Scriptures noted NLT are taken from the *Holy Bible, New Living Translation*, copyright © 1996. Used by permission of Tyndale House Publishers, Inc., Wheaton, Illinois 60189. All rights reserved.

Scriptures noted THE MESSAGE are from *The Message*. Copyright © 1993, 1994, 1995, 1996, 2000, 2001, 2002. Used by permission of NavPress Publishing Group.

Scriptures noted KJV are taken from the *King James Version* of the Bible.

FaithWords
Hachette Book Group USA
1271 Avenue of the Americas, New York, NY 10020
Visit our Web site at www.faithwords.com.

The FaithWords name and logo are trademarks of Hachette Book Group, USA.

Printed in the United States of America.

ISBN: 0-446-54517-1
ISBN-13: 978-0-446-54517-4

LITERARY DEVELOPMENT AND DESIGN:
Koechel Peterson & Associates, Inc., Minneapolis, Minnesota

Joyce Meyer's Portrait Photography
Dario Acosta

living life on a whole

New Level

Each of us has been endowed with the tremendous gift of the freedom of choice. And with every choice we make, there are consequences. I believe there are three main choices that are constantly before us: the choice to be lazy, the choice to be mediocre, and the choice to be excellent.

While most people are stuck in the "mire of mediocrity," those who pursue a life of excellence find the real rewards. They live life on a whole new level, experiencing true fulfillment and satisfaction that many others miss out on.

{ Wishing things will change never changed anyone. }

In order to cultivate a desire to come up higher and be the best we can be, we need to define the differences between being lazy, mediocre, and excellent. Although we may not fit entirely into a single category, we all have room for improvement.

Leave the Lower Level of Laziness

Of the three choices, laziness is the most destructive. King Solomon observed: "I went by the field of the lazy man, and by the vineyard of the man void of understanding; and, behold, it was all grown over with thorns, and nettles were covering its face, and its stone wall was broken down" (Proverbs 24:30–31).

A lazy man does just what he feels like doing, which is usually nothing. He wants everything to be easy. As a result, he winds up going through life unhappy and usually filled with jealousy, envy, and resentment over what others have. He is normally not alert, doesn't plan ahead, and fails to take care of things.

Most of us have a lazy attitude in certain areas of our lives—we're passive instead of active in the way we deal with things. We recognize we have problems or weaknesses, but we haven't committed ourselves to change.

The only way to see this mind-set change is to recognize what we are doing wrong and submit ourselves to the inner working of the Holy Spirit. We must take hold of God's Word and apply it to our lives day after day, situation after situation. In time, *God* will faithfully bring about the necessary change.

Cut Out the Mediocre

All of us wrestle the temptation to accept the mind-set that says, "I'm okay—I'm just as good as anyone else. Besides, everybody is doing it." This mediocre type of thinking plagues the majority of our lives.

Mediocrity means "average, status quo, moderate to low in quality." The mediocre man is neither really bad nor really good—neither worse nor better than others. He is halfway between failure and success and, as a result, frustrated and unfulfilled. He does just enough to get by.

Mediocrity may be acceptable in society, but average people are not remembered. Think about it. The heroes found in history books and the Bible are people who did extraordinary things. They went above and beyond what was expected. If we want our lives to make an impact on those around us, we have to choose to move beyond mediocrity and become people of excellence.

Become a Person of Excellence

A person who is excellent is one who exceeds the status quo. People of excellence do what is right even when no one else is around because they realize that God sees everything. Excellence should be seen in everything we do—our conversation, our dress, the way we care for our home and car, the way we treat people, and so on. So whatever task we work at, we need to "work at it heartily (from the soul), as [something done] for the Lord and not for men, knowing [with all certainty] that it is from the Lord [and not from men] that [we] will receive the inheritance . . ." (Colossians 3:23–24).

The fact is, you and I do not serve an average God. We serve a God of excellence—one Who does exceedingly and abundantly above all we could ask or think. As His representatives, we are called to show forth His character in everything we do. And with that call, we have been equipped with His Seed of greatness—the Creator Himself is living on the inside of us, giving us the power to be extraordinary people.

Excellence is not perfection, but it means we choose to have an excellent spirit. There are rich rewards for those who choose to have an excellent spirit. The Bible says that "Daniel was distinguished above the presidents and the satraps because an excellent spirit was in him, and the king thought to set him over the whole realm" (Daniel 6:3). This is the kind of attitude that says, "I'll do whatever you need, however you need it, and whenever you need it done." The person with an excellent attitude takes what he has and does the best he can with it.

The Choice Is Yours

God ordains a destiny for each of us, but just because He ordains it doesn't mean it is automatically going to happen. It is up to us to cooperate with the Holy Spirit and make right choices, and the choice to walk in excellence is extremely important.

Wherever we are right now in our lives is the result of a series of choices. I realize that as children, other people made choices for us that may have been unwise or damaging. However, just because we started out somewhere doesn't mean we have to finish there. God doesn't show partiality—He sets the same opportunities for success before everyone (Romans 2:11). His promises are available to *whosoever* will believe and obey His Word.

Today, I challenge you to draw a line separating you from your past and make the choice to move forward as a person of excellence. Surrender your soul—your mind, will, and emotions—to God, and let Him give you His grace to *see* and *choose* the more excellent ways. Start doing what you know in your heart is the better thing to do. Choose to be a person who will go the extra mile—a person of excellence!

{ If you want your life to change, your choices must change, and today is the best day of your life to begin. }

{Discover Your True Identity}

Each one of us is a rare, one-of-a-kind person, with a God-given destiny to fulfill—a unique call that only we can carry out. But in order to reach our full potential and truly succeed in life, we must learn to accept ourselves for who we are.

The foundation for success is knowing who we are in Christ. This is our true identity. This understanding comes through learning what God says about us in His Word and then getting our mind and mouth in agreement with it. As you and I begin to think and speak the things that God says about us instead of focusing on our weaknesses, we will find the freedom to be ourselves and be the best we can be in all areas of our lives.

My self-worth is not in what I do—it's in what Jesus did.

The Difference Between Your "Who" and Your "Do"

Growing up in my family, I was conditioned to believe that the better I behaved, the more love and acceptance I would receive. Because my thinking was performance-oriented, I had a poor self-image and became negative about everything and everybody, including myself.

I brought this mind-set into my relationship with God, thinking the more I obeyed, the more God would love and accept me. But I was never able to act right all the time, so I was constantly working and striving to overcome my weaknesses and be *good enough* for God's standards. I was weary, worn-out, unhappy, and lacked self-worth much of the time.

I cried many tears for many years, thinking I was a failure. But God, in His mercy, gave me a clear understanding of 2 Corinthians 5:21: "For our sake He made Christ [virtually] to be sin Who knew no sin, so that in and through Him we might become . . . the righteousness of God [what we ought to be, approved and acceptable and in right relationship with Him, by His goodness]."

I finally began to understand that my self-worth is not in what I *do*—it's in what Jesus *did*. There is nothing you and I can do to *work* our way into right relationship with God (Ephesians 2:8–9). When we are born again, God looks at us and sees the righteousness of Christ, not everything we've done wrong.

God doesn't want us to trust or base our value on our physical appearance, talents, education, job, children, friends, religion, or anything else.

Even when we make mistakes, Jesus understands our weaknesses. He was "tempted in every respect as we are, yet without sinning" (Hebrews 4:15), so He knows what we're up against. If we do something wrong, all we need to do is ask Him to forgive us and wash away our sin with His blood (1 John 1:9). He is not waiting for us to have a perfect performance before He answers our prayers. All He wants is for us to love Him with our whole heart and desire to do His will.

If God approves of us, knowing all the wrong we will ever do, you and I have no right to disapprove of ourselves.

Line Up Your Mind and Mouth with the Master

God wants us to get our minds and mouths in agreement with His Word. This is a key to developing the confidence in Christ we need to succeed. Psalm 119:11 says, "Your word have I laid up in my heart, that I might not sin against You." And Jesus said, "Out of the abundance (overflow) of the heart his mouth speaks" (Luke 6:45).

Satan knows we believe what we *think* and *say* about ourselves more than what anybody else says about us. He wants us to always think and talk about all our failures and weaknesses rather than thinking about God's Word. If we accept the condemning thoughts of the enemy, we cannot walk in the confidence of who we are in Christ.

Instead of receiving the accusations of the enemy, we need to cast them down

with the truth. When Satan brings his thoughts of condemnation, we can say, "There's no condemnation to those who are in Christ Jesus. God loves me, and as far as the east is from the west, so far has He removed my sins from me." When you and I meditate on and speak God's Word, Satan's lies will be swallowed by truth, and our confidence in Christ will increase.

You Can Do All Things Through Christ!

God wants us to find our worth and place our confidence in Christ alone. Apart from Him, we can do nothing (see John 15:5). But we "can do all things through Christ which strengtheneth" us (Philippians 4:13 KJV).

Accept yourself in spite of your weaknesses—God does. Make the decision to get your mind and your mouth in line with His Word. Start proclaiming the positive promises of Scripture over your life, and you'll discover that His grace to succeed is all you need!

{steps to action: James 1:22}
Be doers of the Word, and not hearers only.

IN WHAT AREA OF YOUR LIFE DO YOU WANT TO LIVE ON A WHOLE NEW LEVEL?

....
....
....
....
....
....
....

HOW WILL YOU MAKE THE CHANGES NECESSARY TO BE THE BEST YOU CAN BE?

....
....
....
....
....
....
....

SEARCH GOD'S WORD AND WRITE OUT SCRIPTURES THAT HELP YOU THINK POSITIVELY.

....
....
....
....
....
....
....

IF SOMEONE ASKED YOU WHO YOU ARE, HOW WOULD YOU DEFINE YOURSELF?

....
....
....
....
....
....
....

12 KEYS

to Looking & Feeling Great

Now is the time to begin making *changes* in your life. Don't settle for *feeling* bad one more day while you do nothing except complain. Start *doing* the *little* things each day to *care* for your body and *soul*.

My conference ministry puts me in contact with a great number of people, and I am dismayed by the high percentage of people I meet who are not taking care of their physical bodies. Many of them clearly feel terrible. Anyone can see this in the way they look and the way they carry themselves. You simply cannot look really great if you don't feel great.

I know that's true because for most of my life I did not take care of my body. After years of abuse and stress, I started experiencing serious physical symptoms. In addition to a severe hormonal imbalance resulting in a hysterectomy, I was diagnosed with breast cancer in 1989 and later started having migraine headaches. I was so tired that when I woke up in the morning, I wished it was time to go to bed. I did my duty—I worked hard and kept ministering, but I didn't enjoy anything. Sound familiar?

Out of desperation, I finally began to learn the principles I needed to know to take care of myself. It took a few years to fully recover, but I feel better and have more energy now than ever before—and I'm in my sixties! I came up with a 12-key plan that incorporates what God has shown me over the years to help me look and feel great. I believe they will encourage you to get started making changes that will help you look great and feel great too.

1 Let God Do the Heavy Lifting

Will power and discipline are important, but will power alone will not be enough.

Jesus said that apart from God we can do nothing (John 15:5). Learn to depend on God, asking Him regularly to supply the ability to make right choices. He has not created us to function well without Him, and the sooner we learn that, the better off we will be.

God has a great future planned for you, and you need to be ready for it! You can look great and feel great—ready to do whatever God asks of you.

2 Learn to Love Your Body

When you are feeling fat, ugly, or unattractive, make a decision to do something nice for yourself. Buy yourself a flower or some small thing you like and remind yourself: "I'm created in the image of God. He loves and approves of me, and I will love and approve of myself."

3 Master Your Metabolism

To give your metabolism a boost, try drinking a glass of cold water—it raises metabolism 30 percent. Eat protein and whole grains at breakfast and don't skip meals. Exercising vigorously for ten minutes will also raise your metabolism.

4 Exercise

Daily, moderate exercise cuts your risk of heart disease, diabetes, and stroke in half and melts about twenty pounds a year off your frame. It will also relieve mild depression and make you more productive. Exercise does not have to be strenuous to be effective.

5 Balanced Eating

When you are wavering between healthy or unhealthy food choices, call on the Holy Spirit to help you select the right one. Say out loud, "I have self-control, and I will eat what's best for me." Remember, you only have to make the right choices *one meal at a time*. Maximize your veggies. When ordering out, go for a veggie option or a salad or a tuna or turkey sandwich without cheese.

6 Water Your Life

If you're feeling lethargic and tempted to eat snacks or drink caffeine, try having a glass of water first. The run-down feeling of dehydration is often mistaken for hunger or low energy. Wait fifteen minutes and see if you feel better. Have a glass of water a half hour before every meal and keep a bottle of water with you.

7 Mindful Eating

Keep healthy, snack foods within easy reach: baby carrots, protein bars, raw broccoli, and fresh fruit are good choices. Always ask yourself if you really need food before you eat. Slow down and eat only what is necessary. Never take seconds.

8 Curb Your Spiritual Hunger

If you are feeling bored, lonely, or depressed, food won't fill that void. Instead of eating, close your eyes and picture God's love pouring into you. After a few moments focusing on God's love, you probably won't be nearly as interested in food anymore.

9 De-Stress

We often reach for food when we are upset or frustrated. Rather than reach for food, try closing your eyes or putting your head down on your desk and counting to sixty, picturing each number in your mind as you count it. Breathe deeply while you do this. Soothing music can also be helpful. Remind yourself that this too will pass.

10 Right Vision

Successful lives are made of successful days. When you feel you will never reach your goals, pause and look back at how far you have come. Go somewhere quiet and envision the life you want. With God's help, decide what you can do today—just today—to get one step closer to that life.

11 Make It Easy

Find ways to take shortcuts to health whenever possible. Exercise while you watch TV. Park your car farther out so you have to walk a little ways. Take the stairs instead of the elevator.

12 Take Responsibility

Don't blame your weight or health issues on your circumstances or your family. You may not be responsible for the events in your past, but you *are* responsible for the choices you make in the present. Learn to say to yourself, "No one can take charge of my life but me. With God's help, I have the power to change…starting today."

thoughts

" I've found that the way my day begins sets the pace for the whole day. If I start the morning in a hurry, everything inside me goes into high gear, and I never seem to slow down or relax the rest of the day. On the other hand, if I slow down and enjoy my morning—spending time with God and not rushing to get dressed and out of the house—the whole day goes better.

The simple truth is our pace of living affects the quality of our lives, and God did not create you and me to rush around and live under pressure day after day. King David said, "O satisfy us with Your mercy and loving-kindness in the morning . . . , that we may rejoice and be glad all our days" (Psalm 90:14). It is unlikely that we will *rejoice and be glad all our days* if we are hurrying through them as fast as we can. Our life is a gift from God, and He means for us to slow down and enjoy it! "

thoughts

Is Your
Rubber Band
Breaking?

We live in a fast-paced society that seems to be placing more and more demands on us with each passing year. People are hurrying everywhere, and they're often rude and short-tempered. Many people are experiencing stress in the areas of finances, marriage, and raising children. There's often mental and physical stress on the job caused by overwork. Many times this type of lifestyle causes health problems—adding even more stress.

The word stress

was originally an engineering term that referred to the amount of force a beam or other physical support could bear without collapsing. Today, the dictionary's definition of *stress* includes "mental, emotional, or physical tension; strain, distress." This is a condition all too familiar to most of us. Almost everyone is under some kind of stress—it's a normal part of everyday life.

God created our bodies to withstand a certain amount of daily pressure, so when we push ourselves beyond our limitations, we begin to experience problems. Are you pushing yourself too hard? Many people live in a perpetual state of overload—always on the verge of collapse. They keep stretching themselves to the limit like a rubber band . . . until one day they snap.

A rubber band has an amazing ability to be stretched to its maximum length and then return to its precise original form, but how many times can it do that without weakening or breaking?

Let's say you're working around the house and break a rubber band while trying to stretch it around something. You can't find another rubber band, so you try to fix the

broken one by tying the ends together. Sometimes in our daily lives, we stretch ourselves beyond our capacity, and we snap like the rubber band. We think we've fixed the problem by simply tying the ends back together. But soon we fall into the same behavior that caused us to break down in the first place.

When a rubber band you've tied breaks again, it usually breaks in a different spot. So you tie the ends together in another knot. In our daily lives, when we keep stretching, breaking, and "tying the ends back together," we begin to feel as though we're tied up in knots—inside and out!

The solution seems simple: get rid of those things that cause stress. That may work for

"You will guard him and keep him in perfect and constant peace whose mind [both its inclination and its character] is stayed on You, because he commits himself to You, leans on You, and hopes confidently in You."

ISAIAH 26:3

a while, but it's not the final solution. It's impossible to totally eliminate all the stress from our lives. Our only answer is to adjust our perspective and change the way we respond to the inevitable stresses of everyday life. Over time with repeated exposure to stress, our lives begin to resemble that worn-out rubber band. Exhaustion—both physical and emotional—begins to take its toll. When stress depletes our bodies, our immune system weakens, and sickness (even depression) can set in.

Ignoring God's laws and His ordained limits for our lives will ultimately cause burnout. You simply can't continue to over-work your mind, emotions, and body without eventually paying the price. Think about these things:

Who sets the pace in your life?

Do you let the pressures and stresses of everyday life drive you toward burnout?

Are you stressed from trying to keep up with everyone else?

Are you living under the stress of competition and comparison?

Are you a perfectionist with unrealistic goals?

I believe we can live stress-free even though we live in a stress-filled world, but it might require some radical decision-making. If your life has become a rubber band all tied up in knots, it's obvious a change must take place. Begin to adjust your perspective to match God's. Seek His peace and His pace for your life. Respect your body. Treat good health as a price-less gift. Don't waste the energy God has given you on stress. Save it for living and enjoying life!

priorities

" having a positive attitude not only takes the limits off what God can do in and through us, it also helps us see our circumstances from God's perspective and enables us to enjoy our everyday lives. "

the power of a positive attitude

I believe that more than any other thing, our attitude is what determines the kind of life we are going to have. It's especially important to maintain a positive attitude because God is positive. And when we are positive, it releases Him to work in our lives.

My philosophy was, "If you don't expect anything good to happen, you won't be disappointed when it doesn't." Since my *thoughts* were negative, so were my *words*; therefore, so was my *life*.

When I began to study God's Word and trust Him to restore me, one of the *first* things He showed me was that the negativism had to go. I realized the tremendous power there is in being positive in both our *thoughts and words*. When we maintain a positive attitude, God makes even the things the enemy means for our harm to work out for good for us as well as for the good of others. My own life is a perfect example.

The enemy's plan was to use the years of abuse I suffered to destroy me. If I had chosen to continue responding to my circumstances with a negative attitude of anger and bitterness, he would have succeeded. But instead I chose to be positive and believe God's plan to heal me would come to pass. It did, and now He is helping millions of people through my testimony!

Being positive was an area of my life where God really had to work with me. Many years ago I was an extremely negative person. So many devastating things had happened to me that I was afraid to believe anything good could ever happen.

A Positive Attitude
Takes the Limits Off

You and I *always have a choice* about what our attitude will be toward the life we live. When we decide to react to our circumstances with a negative attitude—such as self-pity, resentment, or bitterness—it hinders God from doing everything He wants to do in our lives and keeps us from reaching our full potential.

For instance, I used to walk into a newly decorated room and when someone would ask, "How do you like my decorations?" I would say, "Well, they look nice, but the wallpaper is loose." I always saw the negative. I had to work a lot harder at having a positive attitude than some people, who just naturally have positive attitudes.

Having a negative attitude did not make me or the people around me very happy. Proverbs 23:7 says, " . . . as he thinks in his heart, so is he." Therefore, if I was a negative person, it was because my thoughts were negative. So I decided that if I didn't want to be negative and unhappy for the rest of my life, I'd have to *think positively,* even if things around me *looked negative.*

Remember the twelve men Moses sent as spies into the land of Canaan? Ten told Moses and the rest of the people about the fortified cities and the giants who lived there. They said, "We are not able to go up against the people [of Canaan], for they are stronger than we are" (Numbers 13:31). The effect of the negative words was amazing—the entire nation of Israel refused to go into the land, thereby forfeiting God's promises to them!

In the same way, a negative attitude can keep you from realizing the promises of God for your life because it keeps you from moving forward in faith. The only two people out of that whole generation who ever saw the promised land were the two spies—Joshua and Caleb—who gave a *positive report.* They said, "Let us go up at once and possess it; we are well able to conquer it" (v. 30). These two men had a different perspective.

> **"** no matter what we face, the truth is ` . . . He Who lives in [you] is greater (mightier) than he who is in the world'
>
> (1 John 4:4). **"**

A Positive Attitude
Gives Us Right Perspective

A positive attitude is a result of focusing on the right thing—God. When we focus on the problem instead of on God, we miss His perspective of our situation. The negative spies said, "There we saw the Nephilim [or giants], the sons of Anak, who come from the giants; and we were in our own sight as grasshoppers" (v. 33). These men *were looking* at the giants and at themselves—they *were not* looking at God.

How does God want us to respond to difficult circumstances? He *does not* want us to ignore them or deny their existence. He just wants us to acknowledge that He is greater than our circumstances and deny their right to control us. Maintaining a positive attitude is one of the most powerful ways we can do that, because it's not our circumstances that make us miserable—it's our attitude toward them.

> **When we keep our eyes on God, we get a whole new perspective about the "giants" in our lives, and we can enjoy our lives while we positively trust Him to take care of our circumstances.**

A Positive Attitude
Helps Us Enjoy Everyday Life

I remember how differently Dave and I dealt with problems in the early years of our marriage. Dave would just go on and do what he normally did—enjoy his life and trust God to take care of it. I, on the other hand, would be worried, frustrated, and upset for days on end. Eventually, we would get an answer, the problem would be taken care of, and I would have wasted a lot of time being upset. I *learned* to choose a positive faith-filled attitude and began trusting God instead of worrying all the time.

Whatever you may be dealing with, I want to encourage you to ask God for grace to maintain a positive attitude all the way through. It will not only help you maintain God's perspective and enjoy your life, but will also make you a blessing to everyone around you. If you let Him, God will use even your problems to create a testimony of His power and goodness.

WHAT IF . . .

{ . . . Henry Ford had listened to Thomas Edison who was *negative* about the idea of a motorcar and tried to get him to give it up to "do something really worthwhile"? }

{ . . . Arnold Schwarzenegger had stopped training to become Mr. Universe when his family pled with him to get a real job and stop "living in a *dream world*"? }

{ . . . In the weeks before she opened her first store, cosmetic tycoon Mary Kay Ash had followed her attorney's advice to "*Liquidate* the business right now and recoup whatever cash you can. If you don't, you'll end up penniless"? }

{ . . . James Michener had believed a New York publisher who told him, "You're a good editor with a promising future in the business. Why would you want to throw it all away to try to be a writer? I read your book. Frankly, *it's not really that good*"? (Michener's first book, *Tales of the South Pacific*, won a Pulitzer Prize.) }

{ . . . Benjamin Franklin had listened to *negative* "experts" who told him to forget about his foolish experiments with lightning? }

dare to dream

Little thinkers
live little lives.

big DREAMS

IT'S IMPORTANT TO THINK BIG WHEN IT COMES TO DREAMS for our future. I recommend you think big thoughts, dream big dreams, and make big plans. We serve a big God who is able to do exceedingly, abundantly, above and beyond all we could ever hope, ask, or think (see Ephesians 3:20). People who cannot conceive of anything beyond what they can see with their natural eyes miss out on the best God has planned for them.

A hope, vision, dream, or plan is like a seed. It is a small thing leading to something big. Everything starts with a seed. We can never have a harvest without a seed, and it's the same way with our dreams. If you have no positive hopes or dreams for the future, you will either stay where you are or begin to slide backward.

The biggest mistake anyone can make is to have no dreams for the *future* and do nothing to make anything in their life better.

Create Opportunities

Some people believe everything in life is a matter of chance. There is nothing they can do about anything except to wait for whatever's going to happen and accept it. It is true that we will have to accept some things we cannot do anything about, but many things can be changed if we pray and do our part. Many dreams can be realized if we only apply the passion and the persistence to realize them.

I used to say, "I'm just not a very creative person," but I don't say that anymore. Now, I pray for God to give me creative ideas, and I confess that I am creative. Have a positive attitude about yourself and your abilities. Just because you have never been a certain way in the past does not mean you can't be that way in the future. It only takes one person with a dream and vision for improvement to light a spark and provoke great change.

Don't wait for some great idea to fall into your mind; instead, search for one. Pray for creative ideas, think about what you would like to do, and then believe you can do it. It simply starts with a dream.

Passivity

Some people have grown up in such difficult conditions they don't even know how to think about getting out. They need to be taught how to think aggressively and take aggressive action.

Passivity is the opposite of activity, and it is very dangerous. A passive person would like to see something good happen, and they sit where they are and wait to see if it does. People who have allowed themselves to become passive have a type of deadness inside them that is frightening. The devil oppresses their will until they are unable to make any decisions or take any action without being moved by an outside force. Passivity is not always, but can be accompanied by, depression, discouragement, self-pity, blame, excuses, and laziness. It takes a lot of determination to break the hold of passivity.

If you have serious problems with passivity in your life, understand that the key to a breakthrough is to trust God and do what you can. Are you doing your part, or just passively sitting around with a bad attitude waiting for someone else to fix your life? God wants to motivate you from the inside. He gives creative ideas, big dreams, and an aggressive, active attitude. God's only gear is forward. He wants you to be decisive, energized by His Spirit, and enthusiastic about life.

Declare out loud you will not just sit in the middle of a mess and waste your life. Declare you are an active, aggressive, creative, passionate person, and you refuse to give up! Initially, you may not feel passionate or aggressive, but you have the ability to make decisions that override your feelings. Your will is the strongest part of your soul, and when you place your will in agreement with God's will, there is nothing in this world that can stop you from succeeding in life.

I DARE YOU:
dream big

1 Think about how great God is and then remind yourself that He is on your side.

2 Make a list of your dreams and don't limit yourself to a certain number. Keep adding to the list as ideas come to you. You'll be amazed at how many of them will indeed come true.

3 Make a plan to pursue at least one of your dreams. Ask yourself what it will take to succeed: Money? Work ethic? More education? A team of people? Once you have a good idea, work hard to make it happen.

4 Dream big, but celebrate the small steps of success along the way. Realize that each effort you make is one step closer to the discipline and dedication required in order to focus your passion for what God's calling you to do.

5 Keep your passion large and in charge of your dreams. Give it your all and refuse to give up.

It is impossible to find God's purpose if you live frozen in fear, unwilling to ever take **chances**. Don't live in fear!

You Cannot Give Birth Until You Conceive

The process of pregnancy is very similar to holding and living out a dream. A creative idea, a dream, or vision formed or imagined in the mind is like a baby conceived in a woman's womb. It is planted as a seed in the heart or spirit of an individual, who goes through a season of pregnancy, labor, and eventual birth. But you're never too young or too old to dream big dreams (see Acts 2:17). You're never the wrong sex or race. The amount of money or education you have doesn't matter. All that matters is your willingness to dream big dreams, to depend on a big God who loves you and wants to see you do great things in life, and to press past all opposition.

Many of the ideas and dreams we have in our hearts reveal the purpose of God for our lives. We sense or feel things, we desire to do things, and it is God's way of showing us our purpose. It is possible to have desires that are not God's will, but if that is the case, He will show you the truth if you're willing to be corrected. Be the kind of person who only wants what God wants, and you won't get into much trouble. I have made mistakes in my life by thinking something I wanted was God's will for my life only to discover my motives were all wrong. God gently corrected me and got me back on the right path, and He will do the same thing for you.

Change Your World

"Preach the Gospel at all times, and when necessary use words."

ST. FRANCIS OF ASSISI

We live in a world that is desperately crying out for help. It's a world where more than 1 billion people live on less than $1 a day . . . where diseases such as AIDS are taking the lives of young and old alike at an alarming rate . . . where nearly sixteen thousand children die from hunger-related causes *every day*. And *right now*, at least two-thirds of the population also does not know Jesus Christ as their Savior and His love for them—more than 4 billion people.

The question is: *Who's going to tell them? Who's going to help them?*

Is Missions Mentioned in the Bible?

We use the term *missions* often in the church, but this word is never actually mentioned in the Bible. *Missions* comes from a medieval Latin word meaning "a task assigned; an act of sending," which is exactly what Jesus did in giving His disciples the *Great Commission*: "Go into all the world and preach the gospel to every creature" (Mark 16:15 NKJV). We, the church, have been given an incredible assignment—the task of evangelizing the world!

The apostle Paul says we are Christ's *personal representatives,* and God is literally making His appeal to the world through us. He goes on to say in 2 Corinthians 5 that we should beg people to be reconciled to God and take hold of the divine favor being offered to them. To be *reconciled* means that we change from being enemies with someone to having friendship. Just think of it—we can help people become friends with God!

When I read this scripture, it grips my heart. I want to make sure I am doing all I

Will you get involved in world missions and commit yourself to bring help and justice to the poor and oppressed?

can to fulfill this high call and take advantage of every opportunity. I regularly ask myself, "What am I doing to help someone else? What am I doing to help people find a relationship with God through Jesus Christ?"

So how do we go about it? Do we all need to be preachers, aggressively sharing the Gospel message? I believe we should always be ready to give a logical defense for the truth of our Christian faith (1 Peter 3:15), but I also believe we *can* and *should* "model" the message. Paul says we should be *living letters* that can be read by all men (see 2 Corinthians 3:2–3). You and I are meant to be living messages!

This means we need to make sure people can *see* Christ shining through our lives. Our attitudes, our actions, and how we treat people always speak much louder than anything we say. Many people have so much pain in their lives that they can't hear what we say until we help relieve their suffering. When we meet people's physical needs and hurts, it opens the door wide for us to address their spiritual needs.

Some are called by God to send, and some are called to go—but *both* are equally important! Every church and every Christian should be involved in helping the poor

and needy. It is a vital part of the Christian lifestyle we are called to live. As we join together, and each of us does what we can, multitudes will be helped and will come to the saving knowledge of God through Jesus Christ.

You Can Change Your World!

More than two thousand years ago, Jesus Christ came to earth and started the greatest revolution this world has ever known . . . *and it is a revolution of love for today*. It's a revolution that takes us outside the four walls of the church and brings us face-to-face with a world that's looking for answers.

I encourage you to carefully consider the following scripture. It's a scripture that, if acted upon, has the power to literally transform your life and, in the process, *change our world*.

"No man has at any time [yet] seen God. But if we love one another, God abides (lives and remains) in us and His love (that love which is essentially His) is brought to completion (to its full maturity, runs its full course, is perfected) in us!" (1 John 4:12).

As Christians, we have a high calling. We've been commissioned by God Himself to reach our world for His kingdom through love . . . and we've been entrusted with the greatest message of all time.

Has God helped you? If He has, pass it on by helping someone else. Let's refuse to do nothing. Let's be Christians the way Christ intended by living a life that speaks for itself. When you give to help other people, your gift may leave your hand, but it will never leave your life.

Don't despair over the discouraging condition of the world! There's one thing strong enough to conquer all the evil in our world today—it's the radical, outrageous, contagious love of God! First John 4:8 says that *God is love.* When we allow His love to flow *to* us and *through* us, the world will see God for who He really is—a Father who desperately wants to have a *relationship* with His children and help them in every situation.

Perhaps you want to help but don't quite know how to go about it. One of the things you can do is join with someone else who is already established . . . someone who is reaching hurting people. Although you may never have an opportunity to travel to a foreign country yourself, you *can* help finance the preaching of the Gospel by supporting ministries and outreaches that relieve the suffering of those less fortunate.

This is my passion. This is my dream. I have dedicated the rest of my life to relieving human suffering and preaching the Gospel of Jesus Christ. I have made a commitment to God that I will always take justice and relief wherever I take His Word. *I've decided to start a love revolution . . . and I am starting with myself. I hope your join!*

Love is not merely a sermon we preach, a theory we discuss, or a feeling we wait to have. It is a decision we make to take action and help someone else have a better quality of life.

{steps to action: Matthew 7:24}

Therefore everyone who hears these words of mine and puts them into practice is like a wise man who built his house on the rock.

ARE THERE ANY "GIANTS" STANDING BETWEEN YOU AND SUCCESS? WHAT CHANGE OF ATTITUDE IN YOUR LIFE WILL DEFEAT THEM?

WHAT IS THE DREAM GOD HAS PLACED IN YOUR HEART THAT YOU NEED TO BRING TO BIRTH? STATE IT AS CLEARLY AS YOU CAN.

ARE THERE NEGATIVE WORDS COMING OUT OF YOUR MOUTH THAT NEED TO CHANGE TO LIFE-GIVING WORDS? WRITE OUT THOSE WORDS AND HOW YOU WILL CHANGE THEM.

DO YOU BELIEVE YOU CAN CHANGE YOUR WORLD? DESCRIBE HOW YOU CAN MAKE A DIFFERENCE.

spiritual maturity

In over thirty years of ministry, I have discovered that even though people may struggle with *how* to pray, they really *want* to pray.

THE POWER OF
simple prayer

{ Prayer is simply talking to God and listening as He talks to us. }

Many of us are longing for a deeper, richer, more dynamic relationship with God through prayer, but when our prayers go unanswered, we begin to struggle with doubt and frustration—we wonder whether we're praying the "right" way, or long enough, or if God is even hearing us.

It's natural to have honest questions about prayer. Even though Jesus' disciples spent a lot of personal time with Him, they still felt the need to ask Him to teach them how to pray (Luke 11:1). He helped them, and when we ask Him, He will help us too.

While there are many aspects to prayer, my desire is to help demystify prayer so you can just *relax and do it*. I want you to actually look forward to spending time doing something that is meant to come naturally . . . like breathing.

PRAYER Is a Personal Matter

Because God has created us as unique individuals, He made us to have an intimate and distinct relationship with Him. Therefore, He will teach us how to pray according to who He has made us to be. Yes, there are principles of prayer that apply to everyone, but God will lead us according to *who we are* and the season of life we are in.

I recall a season in my life when I tried to imitate how other effective Christians prayed, which failed miserably. Fortunately, the Holy Spirit helped me realize that God had a personalized plan for me. I needed to learn what that plan was and follow it, not duplicate someone else's. That is what God wants for you too. He delights in our uniqueness and wants us to be free to express ourselves as we pray.

PRAYER Is Based on Friendship

I believe that the key to effective prayer is approaching God as His friend. When we don't know God as a friend, we lack the confidence to ask Him for anything because we don't feel we've "earned it." When we see ourselves as friends with God, we're more *eager to spend time* talking to Him and *unafraid to ask* for help when we need it.

Becoming friends with God is not difficult. If we are followers of Jesus, He calls us His friends because He has shared with us everything He has heard from the Father (John 15:15). Friendship is based on *sharing*, openly and honestly, and we share

with God *through prayer*. A good relationship with God is not built by emergency prayers when we're desperate. It's based on mutual, regular times of sharing and fellowship.

We develop great friendships by inviting others to be involved in our *everyday* lives, and we develop a friendship with God by sharing our lives with Him throughout each day—recognizing and including Him in our thoughts and conversations as we go about our normal activities. He wants to be involved in *every* area of our lives, whether we're driving our car, walking the dog, or making a meal. God does not have favorites, but He does have intimates. Become one of them!

PRAYER Requires Boldness

As our friendship with God deepens, our prayers will not only grow bolder but also become more effective on behalf of others. In Luke 11:5–8, Jesus shares a story about a person going to his friend's house at midnight and asking for bread. In the *Amplified* version, it says the man got what he asked for because of his *shameless persistence and insistence* to the friend. Similarly, we will only shamelessly persist in prayer when we are in a close relationship with God.

God wants us to be His *close* friends, and He invites us to come boldly before Him: "Let us then fearlessly and confidently and boldly draw near to the throne of grace (the throne of God's unmerited favor to us sinners), that we may receive mercy [for our failures] and find grace to help in good time for every need [appropriate help and well-timed help, coming just when we need it]" (Hebrews 4:16).

{ The more time and energy you and I invest in developing an intimate friendship with God, the more powerful and exciting our communication, or prayer life, will be. }

As you and I become good friends with God, our prayers for others will become more effective and make an eternal difference in their lives too.

PRAYER Blesses Others

The more intimately we know God, the more confident we become in our prayers on behalf of others. When people share their needs with us, we may or may not be able to help them. But we can say, "I'll ask my Friend to help you!" We can actually ask God to do us a favor and help them—that's one of the many benefits of being close to God.

For many years I prayed for my father's salvation and saw no change in his life. I actually came to the very sad place where I thought it was useless to keep on praying. Then God asked me to do a difficult thing—to move my parents close to us and care for them until they died, which we did. Three more years went by, and I still did not see much change in my dad. One morning, I reminded God that I had done what He had asked. Now I was *asking Him for a personal favor*—to draw my father into a relationship with Him.

A few weeks later my dad asked me to come over and see him. At that time he apologized for abusing me and accepted Jesus as the Lord of his life. I believe that because of my friendship with God, my prayers made a difference.

PRAYER Is Exciting and Powerful!

Prayer is simply *talking with God* and *listening to Him*. When you ask Him to teach you to pray, He will answer. Being God's friend is the key to an exciting and powerful prayer life. As you develop your friendship with God by including Him in everything you do, you will grow bold and confident to make requests not only for yourself but also on behalf of others. He stands ready to release His power to bring change in you and the world around you!

Untangle the knots...
one day at a time

PICTURE YOUR LIFE as a jumble of shoestrings all tied up in knots, each shoestring a different color. The different shoestrings represent the different elements of your life, such as your family, your job, etc. This jumble of knots could represent many of our lives—with everything all knotted up. Each knot represents a problem, and the process of untangling those knots and straightening out those problems is going to take a bit of time and effort. It took a long time to tie all those knots, and it will take some time to straighten them all out.

The important thing to remember is, no matter how long it takes, never give up, and never quit—keep at it.

to thank God for the progress you have made thus far and trust Him to lead you to eventual healing—one day at a time.

One of our problems is that in our modern, instantaneous society we tend to jump from one thing to another. We have come to expect everything to be quick and easy. It's difficult for us to have the patience to stick with a problem until we see a breakthrough, and that's why we need God's help. You see, God never gets in a hurry. He never quits or runs out of patience. He will deal with us about one particular thing, and then He will let us rest for a while—but not too long. Soon He will come back and begin to work on something else. He will continue until, one by one, our knots are all untied.

If it sometimes seems that you're not making any progress, it's because the Lord is untying your knots one at a time. It may be hard, and it may take time, but if you will commit yourself to the process of getting well, sooner or later you will see victory in your life and experience the freedom you have wanted for so long. In some

I know from my own experience that it often seems no progress is being made. You may feel you have so many problems that you are getting absolutely nowhere. However, you must keep in mind that even though you have a long way to go, you have also come a long way. The solution is

Promise yourself that you'll stop using your problem as a crutch in your life.

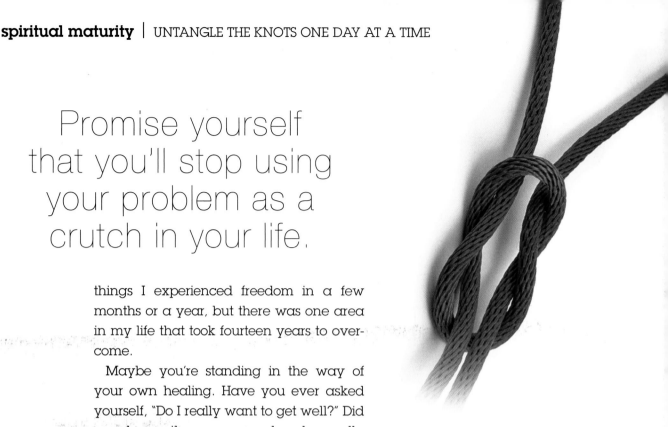

things I experienced freedom in a few months or a year, but there was one area in my life that took fourteen years to overcome.

Maybe you're standing in the way of your own healing. Have you ever asked yourself, "Do I really want to get well?" Did you know there are people who really don't want to get well? It takes some people years to overcome their problems . . . and some never do. They don't really want to move past their problems. It seems they've become accustomed to having those problems around, and they're just content to live with them.

Sometimes people actually get addicted to having problems. It becomes their identity—their life. It defines everything they think, say, and do. Their lives seem to revolve around their problems. If you have a deep-seated and lingering disorder, you may be tempted to make that the focal point of your life. But I encourage you not to give in to that temptation. If you do, it will try to control your thinking and dominate every conversation you have.

If you really want to get well, you'll have to stop using your problem as a means of getting attention, sympathy, or pity. When I used to complain to my husband, he would tell me, "Joyce, I'm not going to feel sorry for you."

"I'm not trying to get you to feel sorry for me," I would protest.

"Yes, you are," he would say. "And I'm not going to do it, because if I do, you will never get over your problems."

That used to make me so mad I could have beaten him to a pulp. We get angry with those who tell us the truth. And the truth is that before we can get well, we must really want to be well—body, soul, and spirit. We must want to get well badly enough that we are willing to hear and accept the truth about our situation.

Make a vow right now that from this moment on you are not going to waste any more of your valuable time feeling sorry for yourself and wallowing in self-pity over things you cannot change. Instead, pledge that you will untangle the knots a little at a time, while living each day to the fullest, looking forward to what God has in store for you as you follow Him . . . one day at a time.

Don't let your life be taken over by your problems.

thoughts

" Do you know that God wants you to believe Him for big things—things you haven't even thought about? There are places God wants to take you—beyond what you have known. And the *only way* to get there is by believing, in spite of how amazing it may seem or how much resistance the enemy sends your way in the form of fear and doubt. "

secrets to trusting God

Faith is the leaning of the entire human
personality on God in absolute trust
and confidence in His power,
wisdom, and goodness.

HAVE YOU EVER looked at someone whom you think has great faith and said, "Wow! I wish I had faith like that!" This may come as a surprise, but if you believe in Jesus Christ, you have all the faith you need to do whatever He wants you to do.

God's Word tells us that He has given a certain amount of faith to everyone (see Romans 12:3). So faith, or trust, is something each of us has and exercise all the time—we cannot function in this world without it. Our faith may be in ourselves, in other people, or in a chair we trust enough to sit down on. The question is: *What are we choosing to place our faith in?*

As believers, God's Word makes it clear that our faith should be in Him and Him alone. Jeremiah 17:7 says, "[Most] blessed is the man who believes in, trusts in, and relies on the Lord, and whose hope and confidence the Lord is." The truth is, our relationship with God and our whole way of life is based on our ability to trust Him. We are also told that the just, or righteous, man will *live by faith* (see Romans 1:17; Habakkuk 2:4).

The key is learning to take steps of faith over time and, through life's experiences, to use what we've been given and cause our faith to grow.

Steps of Faith

Faith operates in a realm that is beyond human reasoning. It's *the substance of things hoped for, the evidence of things* we can't see, touch, hear, or feel (see Hebrews 11:1). So when God speaks to us to do something that requires faith, we need to

do two things. First, we must *choose to trust* God regardless of what we perceive with our senses, and, second, we need to *step out and obey* Him. We can't do one without the other and expect the right results.

In fact, stepping out and obeying *without* trust is what causes many failures. It's foolish to pretend to have faith when we do not. If we are struggling to trust God, we need to be honest and ask Jesus to help as the centurion did, "Lord, I believe! [Constantly] help my weakness of faith" (Mark 9:24), and He will help us.

The greatest honor
we can give God
is to trust Him.

But this does not mean that we won't have to stretch our faith at times. Often we have faith that we haven't been using, and we need to exercise it even though it's uncomfortable for us. Part of my preparation for ministry required quitting my job when God made it clear. *Not* going to work was one of the hardest things I ever did. It meant trusting God to bring in the money I wasn't earning to help pay our bills. It was during that time of stretching I learned to trust Him for everything.

Just because something is hard does *not* mean it isn't God's will. In Luke 5:1–6, Jesus instructed the disciples to come out into the deep and get ready for a large haul of fish. In order to catch all God had for them, they had to take steps of faith that stretched them beyond their comfort zone. The same thing holds true for us.

Time and Experience

Trust is not something we learn to do automatically. It is developed over time and through experience. Even Jesus had to learn faithful obedience *through* His experience. Hebrews 5:8 says, "Although He was a Son, He learned [active, special] obedience through what He suffered." We don't just learn to trust God all at once. He doesn't want us to just trust Him *for* things—He wants us to trust Him *through* things.

The problem is that we have *our way* and *our timing* and God has *His*. And God's timing often includes more waiting than we like. During the wait, we often get confused and frightened, and the enemy attacks us with doubt and unbelief. It's very important that we cast our care upon the Lord and keep believing while we wait on God's timing for good things to come into our lives (1 Peter 5:7).

Only Believe

Whether you are being challenged to take a step of faith or being stretched in a time of waiting, the thing you must do is, *only believe!* (Mark 5:36; Luke 8:50). In every situation remember the words of Jesus: "if you believe, you will see the glory of God" (John 11:40 NASB).

Don't be discouraged if your trust in God seems small. As you continue to use it, your faith will grow beyond what you ever thought possible. Just remember, faith grows over time and with experience—if you will *only believe*.

Even if things don't happen the way we would like them to or when we want them to, we can choose to keep on believing no matter what—*because God is faithful.*

“ Without a healthy attitude toward money and possessions, everyday life can be miserable. People who think too highly of finances and material goods often live in pursuit of luxuries that leave them unsatisfied. They find themselves with full bank accounts and empty hearts. They are driven to earn more, buy more, and have more.

I have no problem whatsoever with people who have nice things. I have some nice things, and I enjoy them, but I am determined not to love them. The money and things we have on earth are for us to enjoy and use to bless others. They are not to make us feel superior to someone else, to hoard or protect, or to show off. We are not to love, treasure, or serve things; we are to love and serve God. We are not to seek things above all; we are to seek God's kingdom first and foremost—and things will be added to us (Matthew 6:33). ”

thoughts

"Most folks are about as happy as they make up their minds to be."

ABRAHAM LINCOLN

Enjoy
[your everyday life]

The only life you can enjoy is your own.
That may seem so obvious it's unnecessary, but think
about it. One of the primary reasons many people do not
enjoy their lives is that they are not happy with the lives they
have. Instead of embracing the realities of their lives, these
people spend their time thinking, *I wish I looked like her. I wish I
had his job. I wish I were married. I wish my marriage weren't so
difficult. I wish I had children. I wish my children would
grow up. I wish I had a new house…*

Accept Your Appointed Lot

The first step to enjoying our everyday lives is to accept the lives we've been given. We must not allow jealousy or comparison to cause us to be absent from our own lives because we want someone else's life.

Wise King Solomon wrote: "Behold, what I have seen to be good and fitting is for one to eat and drink, and to find enjoyment in all the labor in which he labors under the sun all the days which God gives him—for this is his [allotted] part. Also, every man to whom God has given riches and possessions, and the power to enjoy them and to accept his appointed lot and to rejoice in his toil—this is the gift of God [to him]" (Ecclesiastes 5:18–19).

Notice the words *allotted part* and *appointed lot*. Solomon is basically saying, "Take your *appointed lot* in life and enjoy it." In other words, embrace the life—the personality, the strengths and weaknesses, the family, the resources, the opportunities, the physical qualities, the abilities, the gifts, and the uniqueness—God has given you.

Maybe you struggle with challenges that other people do not seem to have. For example, you may have a physical handicap or a learning disability. Perhaps you wanted to go to college, but could not. Maybe you feel you were given fewer abilities or gifts than someone else. You may wish something were different about your spouse, your children, your job, or your financial situation. Whatever the case, you have to take what you have and decide that you are going to do the best you can with it. After all, your life will not change until you start doing so.

God is asking you to be faithful with your life, not with someone else's. In Matthew 25:14–30, Jesus tells the parable of the master who gave three men talents (a type of money)—varying amounts according to each man's ability. Two of the men invested wisely, doubled the master's money, and received the master's commendation, "Well done, good and faithful servant." But the man who had only one talent was rebuked severely for doing nothing with what he had been given. The lesser number of talents he was given had nothing to do with the reward he would have received had he been faithful with what he had.

God only holds us accountable for our gifts and our life, not anybody else's. What are you doing with what you have been given?

> Take the first step toward learning to enjoy your everyday life by making the most of your life. Embrace your life, because God is never going to give you someone else's!

Don't complain; don't compare; don't covet someone else's life, and don't spend your valuable time wishing things were different.

Make the Best of What You Have

Wishing we had what others have is a waste of life. For instance, I *really* wish my hair was easy to manage like my friend's hair. My hair has to be washed and spritzed and dried and sprayed and all sorts of things. But wishing will not change my hair! I have to be happy with what God has given me.

Likewise, you have to be happy with your life. God has given you everything He has for a purpose. Everything about you is by His design. I am not encouraging you to settle for situations that need improvement, but I am urging you to accept the way God made you and the life He has given you. Every life includes good and bad, easy and difficult, strength and weakness. Your life is really no different than anyone else's when you look at it from a broad perspective. There may be specific differences, but nobody has the perfect life.

Embrace the Ordinary

Another key to true happiness lies in understanding that most of life is "everyday." Most of our lives consist of a routine—an unremarkable series of events that take place day after day. So if we are going to enjoy every day, we must learn to embrace the ordinary—to delight in little things, to appreciate small blessings, and to find pleasure in the circumstances and situations other people might overlook.

When I speak of enjoying each day, I am not talking about entertaining ourselves from daylight until dark or about getting "our way" all the time. And enjoying life means more than celebrating special occasions, getting raises and promotions, going on vacations, buying something new, or closing a significant business deal. The truth is: life is not one big party. Noteworthy things do happen, but they are few and far between. We must be able to find joy in going to work, cleaning house, raising children, and paying the bills. To really learn to enjoy everyday life begins with making a decision to do so, because no matter what kinds of lives we have, we will not enjoy them unless we decide to do so.

Much of life takes place when no one is looking; and God works in our lives during the ordinary times. When nothing remarkable seems to be taking place and everything is "business as usual," that's where we develop character and the ability to enjoy everyday life. And as we enjoy life moment by moment, we find all of life has become rich, deep, and satisfying.

True life is really not found in arriving at a destination; it is found in the journey.

How to Handle Your Finances

AMERICANS ARE EXPERIENCING AN EPIDEMIC OF MOUNTING PERSONAL debt. Unfortunately, few of us are taught how to handle our finances by our parents or schools, and even church leadership rarely gives practical instructions about the wise management of our money (although they usually stress the importance of tithing and giving).

How we handle our finances is tremendously important. God is well aware that money is a major part of our lives. Jesus talked about it in the Bible over and over. In fact, there are more than two thousand verses in the Bible concerning money and at least half of the parables of Jesus address the subject.

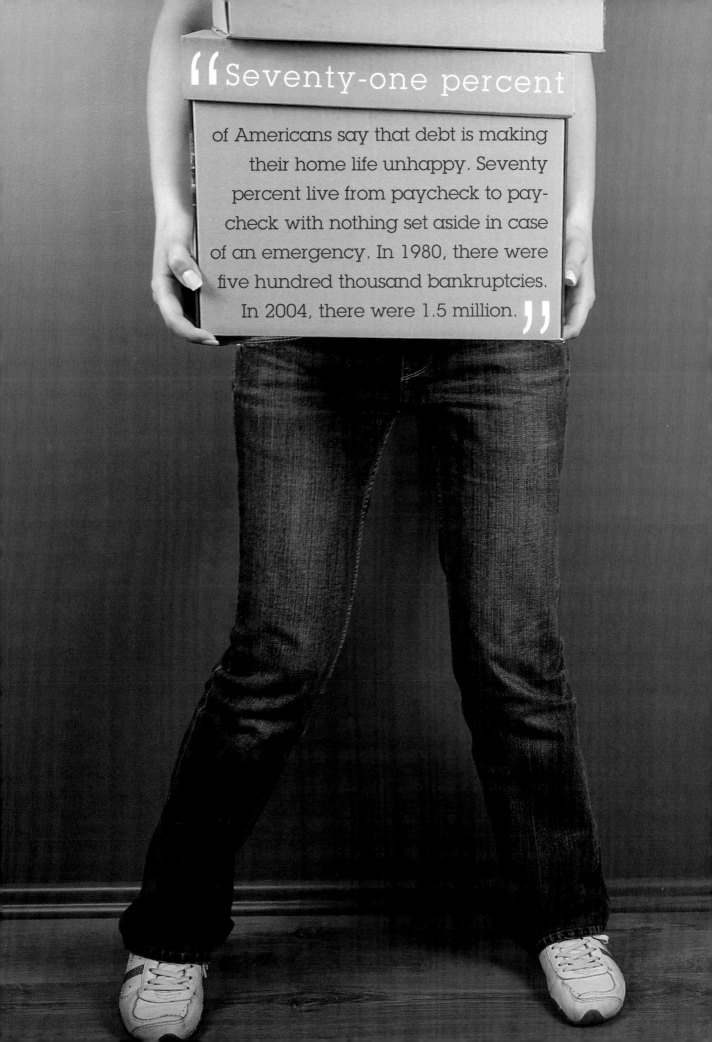

"Seventy-one percent of Americans say that debt is making their home life unhappy. Seventy percent live from paycheck to paycheck with nothing set aside in case of an emergency. In 1980, there were five hundred thousand bankruptcies. In 2004, there were 1.5 million."

If we are **faithful** with little things, God will make us ruler over much (see Matthew 25:21).

Money Is a TEST

In Mark 12:41, we read that Jesus watched what people gave in the offering at the temple. I believe God watches us closely to see how we handle our money *before* He releases more of it into our lives. Jesus said, "if you have not been trustworthy in handling worldly wealth, who will trust you with true riches?" (Luke 16:11 NIV). In this, He was referring to spiritual treasures, such as wisdom, revelation of God's Word, or even a call to ministry.

There are two money tests we must pass. One is how we act when we don't have enough. The other is how we act when we have a lot. God tests us by degrees or levels. Will we hoard it or spend it all on ourselves? Will we give God and others what He tells us to? If we are faithful on one level with a certain amount of income, He will promote us to the next level.

God is trying to get us in a position where He can give us more. God is looking for faithful people who can be trusted with earthly riches as well as the true riches of His kingdom. Why? Because He *wants* to bless us and use us to bless others.

Sometimes God will test us by putting us in a position where we need to trust Him for a financial miracle. When God first called me into ministry, I left full-time work to study and prepare for ministry, which meant our family had a shortage of income every month. For six years we needed a financial miracle each month just to pay our bills. If we needed anything extra, such as clothes or housewares, we prayed and believed God to help. Again and again, God was faithful to provide whatever we needed.

The Power and Importance of GIVING

God can use us to be a blessing to others in many different ways, including using our money to bless others. Proverbs 28:27 says, "He who gives to the poor will not want, but he who hides his eyes [from their want] will have many a curse." When we give to and bless others, we ourselves shall be refreshed (see Proverbs 11:25). If you are generous, open, and willing to give to others as the Lord prompts you, you will never run out.

God wants us to be a channel not a reservoir. You and I are called to give, and we should use what we have to be a blessing to others. If you don't have money, look around your house for things to give away. God's Word tells us that whatever we give in this lifetime we will receive back a hundredfold in eternity *and* in this life (Luke 18:29–30).

Live Within Your BORDERS

One of the things my husband, Dave, taught me is that we need to do four things to be blessed financially. We need to work, give, save, and spend—in that order. If we do these things within the financial limits, or borders, of what we have, those borders will begin to expand.

However, if we crave to be rich and fall into the temptation of chasing after wealth and things, we will be subject to many foolish desires that cause destruction in our lives (1 Timothy 6:9). When this happens, we live outside our borders—spending too much, giving and saving too little, and not working as we should. This puts pressure on our borders and causes them to shrink.

If we are irresponsible with our finances, eventually it *will* catch up with us. However, when we live within our borders—working, giving, saving and spending in a balanced way—our borders will expand.

RESPECT Money, Then EXPECT Money

If you want to see a breakthrough in the area of your finances, you need to start managing well what you have right now. You and I should not *expect* more money from God if we do not *respect* what He has already given us. Taking care of what we already have is a mark of our character.

Money has power and needs to be respected. Having a wrong attitude toward money and using it foolishly leads to oppression and bondage. It can even hinder fulfilling the call of God on our lives. If you and I will submit ourselves and our resources to God, He will show us how to use our money wisely—creating wealth and being a great blessing to others (see Deuteronomy 8:18).

Store Up Treasures in HEAVEN

Being debt-free and learning to manage your money wisely takes effort and even times of sacrifice to see it happen. Seek God's kingdom first and let Him add the *things* to you that you need (Matthew 6:33). Save a portion of your money and make wise investments, but don't put your security or confidence in your money. Instead, take God's counsel and store up treasures in heaven where nothing can destroy them (Matthew 6:19–21). As you seek God with all your heart, He will see to it that money and things come upon and overtake you (Deuteronomy 28:2). You have His Word on it!

Ask God to teach you what you need to know to use your money the right way and to give you the grace to stick with the plan He gives you, no matter how long it takes.

four steps to freedom from debt

It can take as much as five years of living beyond your means before it catches up with you.

THERE ARE CERTAIN MESSAGES in the Bible that apply to everything—*self-control* is one of them. No matter what kind of problem we have in our lives, self-control comes into play. If we don't discipline ourselves, our emotions will rule us, and our lives will be miserable.

To exercise self-control is to live in moderation. Everything good in life requires quality decisions and discipline to make it happen, including how we handle our

Keeping track of your progress is a great encouragement to continue making any sacrifices you need to until you are debt free.

finances. Many of us live under great pressure due to debt as a result of not disciplining our spending habits. If we have gotten ourselves into a mess financially, we are going to have to make a decision to do whatever it takes to get out of it.

Step Two:
KNOW YOUR FINANCIAL STATE

Proverbs 27:23 says, "Be diligent to know the state of your flocks." Many people who are in debt don't know how much they owe or to whom they owe it. Knowing specifically how much we owe and how much we own, or earn, is vital to getting out of debt.

Make a list of all your income and your outgoing expenses. Set up a simple monthly form, or balance sheet, with all your expenses on one side and income on the other. Expenses include regular bills, such as rent or mortgage, utilities, car payments, food, and the amount you are paying on your debts each month. Add up the total for each column of numbers. Is there enough coming in to cover what is going out?

Step One: SET YOUR MIND

Make a decision that you *can* and *will* do it. Start to verbally declare, "I can get out of debt." Once you set your mind to something you *know* God wants you to do, no devil can keep you from accomplishing it.

However, as believers, if we are not being faithful in giving our tithes and offerings, the Bible says we are closing the windows of heaven over our lives and opening the door for the devourer to bring destruction (Malachi 3:10–11). We must bring God our tithe or we will struggle to find financial freedom no matter how good our plan is.

Step Three: MAKE A PLAN

Once we are tithing and know our financial state, with God's help we can make a plan to begin getting control of our money. If you feel you need professional help, find someone who has been successful in handling their finances and ask them for guidance in making a plan. Write down your plan—it will help you stay accountable for sticking with it. Set up a monthly budget and keep your checkbook balanced each month. Closely monitor how your plan is working.

If you have several credit cards that you need to pay off, make the biggest payments you can on the one with the highest interest while paying the minimum payments on the others. When that one is paid off, add the amount of that payment to the minimum on the next card and continue this process until they are all paid off. You may find you need to get rid of every credit card you own in order to discipline yourself and get out of debt.

Step Four: ALLOW FOR TIME

Remember that you probably did not get *into* debt overnight, and you will not get *out* overnight. Lack of self-control over the long haul is what gets us into debt, and long-term discipline is what will get us out. With each act of discipline you take, you are one step closer to being debt free.

Your situation may seem overwhelming, and you may be very undisciplined, but if you believe in Jesus Christ, you have the Spirit of Christ inside you—complete with the fruit of self-control (see John 14:17; Galatians 5:22–23). I challenge you to start saying, "I have a spirit of discipline and self-control. I will do what God tells me to do and not be controlled by my feelings, even in the area of my finances."

If you will *make up your mind*, gather the necessary information to *make a plan* and stick with it, *over time* you will see the harvest of financial freedom that is God's will for your life.

[the ingredients of success]

Developing an attitude of humility is the foundation for greatness.

I believe that God has placed the desire to be great inside each of us. Whatever you and I do in life, we should make it our aim to be great at it, to be the best at it—whether we're a mom or a dad, a minister, a doctor, a receptionist, or anything else.

In seeking to be great, however, we must understand that God's idea of greatness and the world's idea are two very different things. In Matthew 20:25–26, Jesus explained the difference: "the rulers of the Gentiles lord it over them, and their great men hold them in subjection [tyrannizing over them]. Not so shall it be among you; but whoever wishes to be great among you must be your servant."

To attain greatness in the kingdom of God, we must first take on the characteristics of servants who help us become *great men and women* of God.

Servants Walk in *Humility*

In John 13:4–13, Jesus washed the disciples' feet, which was considered one of the lowest jobs for a household servant, and He instructs us to do the same, saying, "If I then, your Lord and Teacher (Master), have washed your feet, you ought . . . to wash one another's feet" (v. 14). The apostle Paul put it this way: "Let this same attitude and purpose and [humble] mind be in you which was in Christ Jesus: [Let Him be your example in humility:]" (Philippians 2:5). He added that even though Jesus was equal with God, He became a servant (vv. 6–7). To become great, we must choose to follow Jesus' example by humbling ourselves and becoming a servant.

Walk in *Obedience*

Jesus walked in obedience by doing whatever the Father told Him, no matter what the cost. In Philippians 2:8 it says, "He abased and humbled Himself [still further] and carried His obedience to the extreme of death." Jesus set an example of greatness for us by walking in *extreme* obedience and laying down His life to serve others.

You and I may not physically lay down our lives for others. However, every time we choose to resist our fleshly tendencies to be unforgiving, unkind, and impatient, laying down *our lives* to serve others, we take up *our* cross and choose death for *our* flesh, which is what we want, think, or feel. A great man or woman in the kingdom of God makes *obeying* the Spirit of God a habit—regularly choosing God's will over their own desires.

I can honestly say, I don't know if I would be doing what I am *now*, if I didn't do the right thing when I was asked to compromise my integrity *then*.

Walk With *Integrity*

Integrity is vital if we are going to be a servant God can trust. In order to serve others with integrity and honesty, we will have to fight for it. God's Word tells us that although we live *in the world* we are *not of it* (see John 15:19). And the world's ways often include dishonesty and manipulation to obtain places of greatness or leadership. The problem is, if we get into leadership that way, *we* will have to keep our position the same way. On the other hand, if we focus on being a servant, maintain our integrity, and allow God to place us in positions of leadership, *He* will keep us there.

Many years ago I worked for a man who asked me to be dishonest with the bookkeeping. I really struggled with the decision, thinking I would lose my job if I refused, but I chose to do what was right. Although he was irritated with me, he didn't fire me. In fact,

The Way It Works in
God's Kingdom …

If you want to have more, give
away some of what you have.

The first will be last
and the last first.

"Down" is the way "up."
Humble yourself,
and He will lift you up.

Servanthood is the
way to greatness!

I ended up getting several promotions during the time I worked for that company.

Because I chose to walk in integrity, my boss knew he could trust me. God feels the same way about us when we choose to walk in integrity—He can trust us with great opportunities to serve.

Great Attitudes Make Great People

I believe that humility, obedience, and integrity are three key characteristics that contribute to the making of a great man or woman. If you humble yourself before God, develop a habit of obedience, and choose to walk in integrity in every area of your life, you will be well on your way to showing the world *what really makes* a great person great.

relationships

The world is looking for something **real**, something **tangible**—for unconditional love.

The Greatest of These . . .

Loving and being loved is what makes life worth living. Love can melt the hardest heart, heal the wounds of a broken heart, and quiet the fears of an anxious heart. From the remotest parts of Africa to the modern cities of America, people comprehend and are hungry for kindness, warmth, and the caring attitude that is the true trademark of a disciple of Christ.

You and I can devote our time and energy to many things—education, career, and accomplishments of all sorts. But all these things will one day be gone. Learning how to walk in love is an investment that will bring rich rewards both now and for eternity. As Paul said, "Love never fails [never fades out or becomes obsolete or comes to an end]" (1 Corinthians 13:8).

One of the most rewarding things I've discovered is how to *show* love in practical ways—with our thoughts, words, and possessions.

Loving With Thoughts

Every word we speak and every action we take is always preceded by a thought. Our thoughts not only affect others, they also affect us in a most amazing way. Proverbs 23:7 teaches us that "as he thinks in his heart, so is he." If we think *unkind* thoughts, we become unkind. But if we think *loving* thoughts, we become loving. Therefore, we must *choose* our thoughts carefully because they affect us and, consequently, those around us.

There is no way we can think critical, negative thoughts about people and then be loving and kind to them when we are in their presence. If we want to show people the love of Christ, we must first make a decision to think good thoughts about them.

This choice to think right thoughts is an ongoing war that rages on the battlefield of our minds. Second Corinthians 10:5 says we are to cast "down arguments and every high thing that exalts itself against the knowledge of God, bringing every thought into captivity to the obedience of Christ" (NKJV). How do we "cast down" wrong thoughts? As soon as a negative, critical, or judgmental thought presents itself in our thinking, we need to refuse to receive it and refuse to turn it over in our minds.

After the wrong thoughts are cast down, the key to victory is to *replace* them with right ones (Philippians 4:8). When a new thought comes in, the old must go. As you and I allow our thoughts about others to be positive, our attitude and words will follow.

Loving With Words

Our words also have a tremendous impact on our lives and the lives of others. Proverbs 18:21 says, "Death and life are in the power of the tongue, and they who indulge in it shall eat the fruit of it [for death or life]." We must learn to use our words for blessing, healing, and building up and not for cursing, wounding, and tearing down.

Right words produce a harvest of *good* relationships, and wrong words produce a harvest of *bad* relationships (Galatians 6:7). Believing the best of people and speaking words that build them up is one way of loving them. "Pleasant words are as a honeycomb, sweet to the mind and healing to the body" (Proverbs 16:24). It is easy to find something wrong with everyone, but "love covers a multitude of sins" (1 Peter 4:8).

All of us need to make a commitment to love others with our words. Choose your words carefully that they may produce a positive harvest in the lives of others.

Every word we speak can be a brick to **build** with or a bulldozer to destroy.

Loving With Possessions

Now that we have dedicated our thoughts and words to the Lord, the next step is showing love with our actions. First John 3:18 says, "Let us not love [merely] in theory or in speech but in deed and in truth (in practice and in sincerity)."

One of the best ways to show people love is by sharing our personal possessions. There are hurting people everywhere—the poor, the sick, the emotionally wounded, and the lonely. A simple act of kindness such as giving away a pair of earrings, a meal, or spending some time with someone in need can make an individual feel loved and valued.

Like Abraham, we are called by God to be blessed and to *be a blessing*. Genesis 12:2 says, "I will bless you [with abundant increase of favors] and make your name famous and distinguished, and you will be a blessing [dispensing good to others]." The more we use our resources to be a blessing to others, the more God will bless us.

You and I can **learn to love** people and use things—**instead** of loving things and using people to get them.

The Greatest of These Is Love

So where does love fit into our list of priorities? It should be number-one on our spiritual priority list. We should study love, pray about love, and develop the fruit of love by practicing loving others (Galatians 5:22–23). God first revealed and expressed His love through His Son Jesus and is now calling on us to continue this mission. It is the best thing you and I can commit our lives to. We show others Jesus by walking in love (John 13:34–35).

The apostle Paul stated that "faith, hope, love abide…but the greatest of these is love" (1 Corinthians 13:13). Are you ready and willing to become a student of the love walk? If so, it is going to require education and commitment. First Corinthians 14:1 says to "eagerly pursue and seek to acquire [this] love [make it your aim, your great quest]."

I challenge you to find someone who operates in love and study how they handle people and difficult situations. And take it one day at a time. Remember, God is the one who will do the work of renewing your thinking and give you the grace (power) to walk out what you learn. All that is required of you is to be willing to surrender yourself to Him and follow His lead. By loving others with your thoughts, words, and actions, you will soon discover that it not only blesses the receiver, but it also blesses the giver!

are you a People Pleaser?

One of the most freeing things I have ever learned
is how to break free from being a people pleaser.

By *people pleaser*, I mean an individual who spends a good part of his life trying to please other people, who lives under the pressure to perform. It is based on an unhealthy drive to be accepted and approved by others. How other people think and feel about them has become so important it is like an addiction—a desire so strong it influences the majority of their decisions and affects every part of who they are. And its fruit is unhappiness, bitterness, resentfulness, and depression.

Are You Honest With Others?

One of the clearest signs of being a people pleaser is not being truthful with others about who we are. We say we like things we really don't like. We go places and say we are enjoying it, when we hate it. And we nod our heads in agreement to things we don't feel right about in our hearts. Instead of telling people the truth about our desires, feelings, and thoughts, we develop a pattern of telling others what we think they want to hear in order to remain accepted. Whatever the reason, untruthfulness in relationships only leads to heartache.

Ephesians 4:15 says, "God wants us to grow up, to know the whole truth and tell it in love" (THE MESSAGE). Verse 25 goes on to say we are to "put away all falsehood" and "tell our neighbors the truth," because we belong to each other (NLT). God wants us to be truthful with one another at all times in a kind and considerate way.

Do You Do Things Out of Duty or Desire?

People pleasers do things for others out of a sense of *duty* instead of *desire*, feeling obligated or expected to do it. And we are afraid if we don't, others will get mad at us or think badly of us. But doing things because we feel forced or because we fear being rejected is the wrong reason.

Now, please understand that we do not have to "want" to do everything we need to do. There are many things we are required to do, such as getting up for work, that have nothing to do with being a people pleaser. So there is a balance in this area that God will help us find. But we need to get out from under the pressure and expectations of others to do something for them.

Are You Constantly Sacrificing Your Own Legitimate Needs?

A people pleaser is quick to set aside his own genuine needs to meet the needs and wants of others. Each of us has legitimate needs to be loved, accepted, and approved. We also have needs for attention, affection, and rest. Constantly denying our genuine needs and doing things for everybody else will usually result in becoming bitter and resentful because we feel all used up.

Yes, the Bible says we are to live a life of self-denial and even put the needs of others before our own. However, if we are *always* denying our own needs and *always* putting the needs of others before our own, we are out of balance, which opens the door for the enemy to wreak havoc in our lives (1 Peter 5:8).

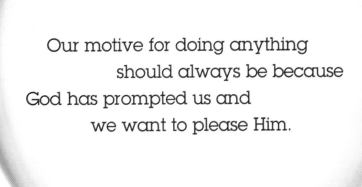

Our motive for doing anything should always be because God has prompted us and we want to please Him.

When I became a committed Christian, I told myself, *I will sacrifice everything—including my own legitimate needs for rest, fun, and friends—for the sake of God's call.* But after I pushed myself beyond my personal limits and got physically sick on at least three occasions, I realized I could no longer neglect my legitimate needs. Since then, God has helped me find and maintain a balance between caring for the needs of others without neglecting my own, and He will do the same for you.

You Can Overcome Being a People Pleaser

There is only one real remedy for being a people pleaser, and that is learning to follow the leading of the Holy Spirit in all that we do. As believers, the Holy Spirit lives inside us, and He desires to lead us in everything we do, from the type of job we have to what we do or don't do for others.

The apostle Paul says, "So now we serve not under [obedience to] the old code of written regulations, but [under obedience to the promptings] of the Spirit in newness [of life]" (Romans 7:6). When we follow the leadership of the Holy Spirit, we experience a peace, joy, and contentment that cannot be experienced when we live under the "shoulds," the "oughts," the obligations, and the expectations of being a people pleaser.

For the most part, the leading of the Holy Spirit means having an inner peace about doing something. Colossians 3:15 says, "And let the peace (soul harmony which comes) from Christ rule (act as umpire continually) in your hearts [deciding and settling with finality all questions that arise in your minds]." In other words, if we have or don't have a peace in our spirit about doing something, we can know the Lord's leading.

> **"** Walk (live and conduct yourselves) in a manner worthy of the Lord, fully pleasing to Him and desiring to please Him in all things. **"**
>
> COLOSSIANS 1:10

It All Comes Down to Motives

Why are we doing or not doing something? Are we motivated by fear, personal gain, or a sense of obligation? Are we motivated by a desire to be in control, accepted, or seen? These are all the wrong reasons for doing something.

Remember, whatever you and I do, if we will do it as unto the Lord, our lives and the lives of others will be blessed—whether it means helping a family member, visiting a friend, or volunteering at church (see Colossians 3:23–24). The result will be a new measure of joy and enthusiasm in your life—even in the everyday, ordinary things.

I encourage you to shake off the way people think or feel about you and begin to do what you feel God wants you to do. If you need strength in this area, pray and ask the Lord for His grace to follow after His voice instead of the pressures and demands of others.

Be a Servant,

Not a Martyr!

WE ALL KNOW WHAT A MARTYR IS. We've all heard heartrending stories of heroic men and women who, down through the ages, have paid the ultimate price and been killed for what they believe. But there's another kind of martyr without courage and nobility. I'm sure we all know one—a great and constant sufferer who's always willing to share their pain with anyone who will listen. This martyr wants everyone around to know the sacrifices they're making in their life.

We lose a lot of blessings we never even know about simply because we fail to do for others what we would like to have done for us. We always want to be blessed in return by the people we bless, but it doesn't always work that way.

I once knew a woman like this. She felt like a slave to her family, and she definitely had the attitude of a martyr. I got so tired of hearing her continually talk about how much she did for everyone and how little anyone appreciated her. I could tell she kept a running account of the work she was doing versus the reward she was receiving for it. Eventually, she ruined her marriage and most of her relationships with her children. What a tragedy!

The Martyr Trap

The "martyr trap" is such an easy one to fall into. We start out serving our families and friends and loving it. But after a while, our hearts begin to change, and we begin to expect something in return. After all, we're working so hard and sacrificing so much.

Eventually, we no longer have the heart of a servant. We become discouraged because our expectations aren't being met. Our attitude sours, and we soon find out we've become mired in self-pity. We've become a martyr.

It can come down to an act as simple as cutting the fruit for a fruit salad for your husband. Who hasn't picked up the knife and thought, *I really don't want to make him a fruit salad. Why do I always have to do this stuff for him? Why doesn't he do things for me?* (If you've never had that thought, know that I have!) And so we begin to chop the fruit with a vengeance, feeling the role of the martyr.

In moments such as these, the Lord has stopped me and said, "Joyce, what I hear you saying over and over is, 'What about me? What about me?' Don't you see that when you are serving Dave, you are serving Me?"

That truth changes everything. Having a terrific marriage relationship is possible, if we are willing to surrender our own way and let God lead us to the pleasant plan He has in mind for us. As we learn to serve God's way, true happiness is found in the joy we feel after ministering to our spouse and family. God anoints us so we can do something to make somebody else's life better. Happiness is found in living a "giving lifestyle."

Love Serves

I wonder how many marriages could have been saved from divorce if husbands and wives had been willing to show love by serving one another. It seems that everyone today wants to be "free," and Jesus has indeed set us free. But He never intended for us to use that freedom selfishly. He wants us to serve others.

I definitely love my husband, and sometimes that love is best expressed through service. Words are wonderful, but when you walk in love, your commitment must contain much more than just words. How can I truly love my husband if I never want to do anything for him?

Make a decision to be a radical blessing to your husband, family, and world of influence. Give away time and love to those who need help, whether or not they have anything to give back to you. Sow seeds that meet their needs, and know that God can give you rewards of peace and joy that you don't even realize.

Start Today

If your marriage, a family relationship, or a friendship isn't what you want it to be, you can literally turn it around by adopting this one principle right now. You may have been waiting for your spouse or child or friend to do something for you. Maybe you have even been stubbornly refusing to be the first to make a move. Swallow your pride and save your relationship. Stop talking about all the sacrifices you make and start serving your loved ones. Make them the focus, not you . . . and be a servant, not a martyr!

"For you, brethren, were [indeed] called to freedom; only [do not let your] freedom be an incentive to your flesh and an opportunity or excuse [for selfishness], but through love you should serve one another" (Galatians 5:13).

{steps to action: Luke 11:28}

Blessed rather are those who hear the word of God and obey it.

ARE THERE PEOPLE IN YOUR LIFE WHOM YOU STRUGGLE TO LOVE? WRITE DOWN THE CRITICAL, NEGATIVE THOUGHTS YOU HAVE THAT MAKE LOVING THEM SO DIFFICULT.

....

....

....

....

....

....

GOD DESIRES TO EXPRESS HIS LOVE THROUGH YOUR LIFE. WRITE OUT A SIMPLE ACT OF KINDNESS YOU WILL DO TO SHOW LOVE TO A HURTING, NEEDY PERSON.

....

....

....

....

....

....

DO YOU FIT THE DESCRIPTION OF A PEOPLE PLEASER? IF SO, WHAT AREA OF YOUR LIFE CAN YOU CHANGE TODAY THAT WILL HELP FREE YOU TO BE WHO YOU REALLY ARE?

....

....

....

....

....

....

HOW CAN YOU HAVE THE HEART OF A SERVANT AND NOT END UP BEING EVERYBODY'S DOORMAT?

....

....

....

....

....

marriage & family

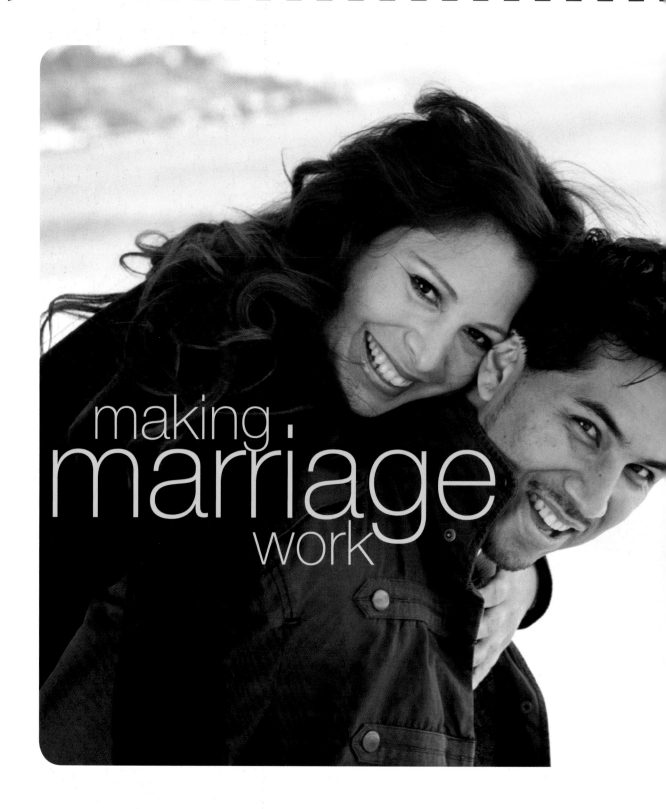

making
marriage
work

Sharing Information

Enjoying Fellowship

Problem-Solving

Lion or Lamb

Confronting in Love

 COMMUNICATION is more than just talking. Our facial expressions, tone of voice, and body language all contribute to what people are hearing us say. We can *mean* to say one thing but *communicate* something entirely different. That is why it is important for us to be sensitive to what we communicate through our actions, not just our words. This is true in all our relationships and crucial in helping to build a strong, healthy marriage relationship.

Sharing Information

Some communication is simply for the purpose of sharing clear information, which helps avoid confusion and misunderstanding and affects the daily plans of the people with whom we live and work with. For instance, when we give little reminders of things to be done, such as attending a son's baseball game, or alert our spouse we will be working late, it lets our spouse know we're being considerate of their time and schedule. Sharing information may not be the most personal form of communication, but it is necessary and paves the way for deeper fellowship.

If we wait for God's timing, we know His power to resolve our conflicts will be present.

Enjoying Fellowship

Some communication is simply for the purpose of fellowship and takes place just by talking *with* each other—a time for a friendly exchange of ideas and conversation. When you and I give our spouse the gift of undivided attention, it fills our need for companionship with each other.

Enjoying fellowship requires both talking and listening. Sometimes I tell Dave, "Just sit down with me while we have a cup of coffee." These are good opportunities to keep the lines of communication open by taking an interest in the things our spouse is involved in, and we grow closer to each other. Spending regular time communicating with our mate at this level can make it much easier to deal with problems when they come up.

Problem-Solving

Communicating to solve problems is indeed a fine art. Conflict is a part of everyone's life, so how we deal with it is important. The inability to deal with conflicts in a Christ-like manner is often a major source of problems in our marriages.

When addressing a conflict, be especially aware of the timing. We can get ourselves into a lot of trouble by either barreling into things without waiting for God's timing or constantly avoiding conflict—even allowing things to continue that we know God is telling us to address. Ecclesiastes 3:7 says there's a time to speak and a time to be silent, so look for the right time to discuss a problem. Learn to pray first by saying, "God, is this the right time?"

Lion or Lamb

You and your spouse need to understand how people with your personality type approach conflict. We need to examine ourselves to see whether we are the type of person who likes to instantly confront, like a lion, or if we are more like a lamb and want to hold back and not deal with issues.

Throughout the New Testament, we see Jesus acting in two contrasting ways. Like a lion, He confronted the moneychangers in the temple and gave them firm correction (Matthew 21:12–13). Like a lamb, He went before the Jewish leaders, falsely accused without speaking one word in His defense (Isaiah 53:7). It's difficult to resist defending ourselves when we have been misunderstood or falsely accused.

Lion personalities, like mine, have to learn to hold back and wait on God. Lamb personalities have to learn to speak up in obedience to God's leading—whether they want to or not.

When we need to communicate with someone concerning confrontational issues, we should pray for God's grace and mercy to anoint us as lion-hearted lambs. Then we need to wait until the Holy Spirit helps us find balance in our perspective and approach to the situation. The key to improvement is learning to confront when God says to confront and to leave an issue alone when He says to leave it alone.

Confronting in Love

Dealing with difficult issues in love is the surest way of enjoying peace in our relationships. First Peter 4:8 says that love covers wrongdoing. In other words, when there is an issue between a husband and wife, deal with it privately. This helps avoid building walls of offense. Bringing up issues in public only serves to humiliate the other spouse. Matthew 18:15 instructs us to go privately to someone who offends us—that is what we would want them to do for us.

Another thing that helps us confront in love is to realize that we have faults of our own. We need to humble ourselves and gently approach our spouse. Our motivation should be to let them see God's great love for them—not to tear them down. A humble and loving attitude expresses correction not only with the purpose of restoring fellowship and peace, but also with a desire to see God bless them and make them more like Christ.

At the Heart of a Good Marriage

The Bible says that the process of a man and woman becoming one is a profound mystery, but it is meant to reveal the heart of Christ for His church (Ephesians 5:31–32). So stop and think about it:

- Does the communication between you and your spouse reflect the kind of love Jesus has for the church?
- Do you love each other by being considerate of your spouse's time and schedule and keeping them informed to help make their life a little easier?
- Are you expressing the love of Christ by just wanting to be with them, talking about what they are interested in, and being willing to share your heart with them?
- Are you showing them God's love by the way you confront them when it is necessary?

Your marriage is meant to be a blessing not only to you but to the people around you. It is one of the ways God creates a picture for people to see how much He loves them. The way we communicate—words, actions, and attitudes—puts the love of God on display for everyone around us. Learn God's way of communicating and you can use your words to help paint a picture of God's love for everyone to see!

When we share our most intimate hopes and concerns with our spouse, we build a mutual trust and admiration that bonds us together.

I ONCE MADE A DISASTROUS MISTAKE and asked my husband, Dave, for the last bite of his hamburger. If there's anything hard for a man to sacrifice, it's that last bite. It's much easier to give somebody the first bite because he still has so much of it left, but when he's down to the last bite, it's tough. I didn't realize before how much of a test it could be, especially for Dave.

Our exchange began as usual, with his offer, "I'm going to stop here and get a hamburger. Do you want one?"

"No, no, no. I don't want anything."

"Are you sure you don't want anything? Let me get you one."

I firmly said, "Dave, I don't want a hamburger."

He said, "I'll eat what's left."

"I *do not want* a hamburger."

"Okay."

He bought a hamburger, and it smelled so good. I waited and waited, trying my best not to ask for a bite of that hamburger. But he got down to the last bite, and I couldn't stand it.

"Do you suppose I could have that last bite?"

Dave got upset with me and said with a huff, "Why didn't you let me get you a hamburger? I'll buy you all the hamburgers you want! Why do you only want to eat mine?"

"It's only one bite!" I defended. "You don't have to be so selfish!"

"*All right!* Here it is."

"Nope, I don't want it! I wouldn't eat that hamburger now! You couldn't pay me to eat that bite of hamburger!"

"You eat this!"

"I'm not eating it!"

"You eat it!"

"I will not!"

"Well, I'm not eating it," Dave replied, "so you might as well."

So I took it, shoved it in my mouth, and chewed it up.

Don't Trade Happiness for a Hamburger

> "Above all things have intense and unfailing love for one another, for love covers a multitude of sins [forgives and disregards the offenses of others]."
>
> 1 PETER 4:8

No Comparison Shopping

I was upset not only because Dave had hurt my feelings, but also because I'd compared the way he treated me to the way I saw other men treat their wives. I said, "Well, other men give their wives bites of their food. I just ask you for *one stinkin' bite* of your hamburger, and you throw a fit!" I was mad for about an hour after that argument.

It takes a little while for the Lord to get through to us when we're enjoying our vengeance and self-pity, just as I was. But finally I started feeling the Lord deep within me saying, "Joyce, you are acting ridiculous. The man told you he would buy you a whole sack of hamburgers if you wanted them."

Dave had offered to buy me a hamburger even if I wanted just one bite of it. He'd clearly asked me in advance not to ask for his. It doesn't matter what other men do. Sharing that last bite of hamburger bothered Dave. When you are comparing your spouse to someone else, remember that person probably has some faults your spouse doesn't have that would drive you crazy and be just as difficult to accept. What's the sense in pushing something on your spouse if it bothers them? Just don't do it.

Let It Go

Marriages are not as good as they could be when people hold on to little things that have hurt or offended them. It's difficult to completely open yourself up after being hurt because you're afraid you'll be hurt again. Nobody can promise that loving someone won't hurt. In fact, you can't love without being willing to be hurt. It's not possible.

You can't have real love unless you're willing to forgive. Love keeps giving the other person another chance. Love keeps trusting them over and over again, expecting them to do the right thing the next time. I realize there are big hurts and also little things we deal with daily. Sometimes we may not even know what is agitating us, but we need to decide to let go of its irritating hold on us.

Ask the Lord to reveal what it was that caused you to feel bitterness or resentment. You may be surprised at what He drags up, but when you see the truth, decide to let go of that grief. Decide to forgive the person who didn't respond to you in the right way.

It took me several days to completely get over the hamburger incident. That's the truth! My feelings had been hurt because Dave didn't want me to have that bite of his hamburger. But I had to get over it and move on. Don't trade your happiness for a bite of hamburger!

Are You Too Busy?

BUSYNESS OR FRUITFULNESS?—THAT IS the question. It's easy to be involved in many different efforts and good causes, but the truth is, busyness does not guarantee fruitfulness. It also does not confirm that we are in God's will. It is the *quality* of what our lives produce that determines whether we are truly fruitful.

Is your **life** full of meaningful accomplishments or just busy activities?

Jesus said that He chose us so that we would bear much fruit (John 15:16). One good way to help determine if you are being fruitful or just busy is by asking yourself some questions, such as:

- Am I spending my time doing what helps fulfill my life purpose?
- Am I doing what I really desire to do?
- Am I using my God-given gifts and talents?
- Am I being controlled and pressured by circumstances and expectations of others?
- Do I see tangible results—good fruit—from my busyness?

If you and I **want** to be fruitful, we need to make spending **time** with Jesus our number-one **priority**.

The Source of Fruitfulness

Being fruitful begins with *putting God first*. As we spend time with Him, He will direct us and give us peace about what we should be doing. Jesus said, "I am the Vine; you are the branches. Whoever lives in Me and I in him bears much (abundant) fruit. However, apart from Me [cut off from vital union with Me] you can do nothing" (John 15:5).

In Luke 10:38–42, we read the story of Martha and Mary. Martha was very busy serving, *even serving Jesus*. She got angry because her sister sat at Jesus' feet listening to Him talk instead of being *busy* helping her serve. Jesus' response to Martha was that Mary had chosen the best thing to do at that time—sit and listen to Him.

Years ago, I was constantly busy like Martha, and eventually it had a bad effect on my relationship with God and others— especially with my husband. I didn't know how to relax and have fun, so it made me very angry when others did. I had to learn not only how to enjoy life but also to make enjoying time with God the *most* important thing in my life.

Good Versus Best

I believe that Satan uses the pressure of busyness to keep us from fulfilling God's purpose for our lives. In many cases, we become distracted by things that are *good*, even "Christian activities," but are not God's *best* for us. We can get so busy we don't even recognize the thing we *should* be doing that is really important.

In order for you and me to avoid this trap, we need to "learn to sense what is vital, and approve and prize what is excellent and of real value [recognizing the highest and the best, and distinguishing the moral differences]" (Philippians 1:10). We need to look to God and ask Him to give us the grace to make wise choices concerning the things we *should* or shouldn't be doing.

Are You Enjoying Your Life?

One biblical way for us to know if we are bearing good fruit is to examine the actual fruit our lives are producing. If we are in God's will, following His Spirit, we will produce the fruit of His Spirit—"love, joy (gladness), peace, patience (an even temper, forbearance), kindness, goodness (benevolence), faithfulness, gentleness (meekness, humility), self-control" (Galatians 5:22–23).

Another way you and I can know we are being *fruitful* is that we will have a sense of accomplishment rather than frustration. I spent many years being out of balance—busy but not fruitful, under pressure and frustrated. Thankfully, God has taught me how to live a balanced life. As you and I learn to direct our time and energy toward the things God has given us to do, we will enjoy our lives more and experience a true sense of accomplishment that only comes from being fruitful.

If you really want to know if you're **operating** in the **fruit** of God's Spirit, ask a trusted friend or family member what kind of things they see operating in **you**.

Destined to Bear Fruit

God's plan for you is to fulfill your destiny, which is to bear much fruit. But if you are too busy to spend time with God and the people around you, you are *too* busy. That's when you need to seek God for the grace and wisdom to make the needed *changes* in your life. He will help you make wise decisions each day and set your priorities right—beginning with the priority of spending time with Him. As you learn to keep God first and exercise godly wisdom in decision-making, you will bear *much fruit* and glorify your Father in heaven.

Loving Who You Are

How do you like yourself? Do you love yourself in a balanced way? I'm not talking about a selfish, self-centered way. God wants you to love yourself, because you are the one person that you are never going to get away from. So you better learn to like yourself. Face it—you're stuck with you!

Come As You Are

The Bible tells us to love our neighbor as we love ourselves (see Matthew 22:39). However, if we don't love ourselves, how can we love anyone else? You and I have to like ourselves and believe that God had something special in mind when He made us. No, we're not perfect, but God didn't make us imperfect. The imperfection is because of sin in the world and its effects on us, which includes bodies that don't always behave right. However, the Bible tells us to come as we are to Jesus (see Matthew 11:28), and He will make us what we need to be.

Me, Myself, & I

I believe the single greatest problem that most people have is that deep down inside, they don't like who they are. I don't mean in a me-me-me kind of way, but loving ourselves as the person God created us to be. The only cure for insecurity is to know we are loved and valued by God, and thus we can love and value ourselves.

When we have problems, we shouldn't run away from God but rather run to Him with our problems.

We need to get our eyes off of everything that's wrong with us as well as everything we think is right with us, because our eyes need to be on Jesus.

Some people think, *Oh, we shouldn't say we love ourselves.* Yes, we should. Why are we so much more comfortable saying, "I hate myself" or "I don't like this about myself," rather than saying, "I like this about myself. I like my personality"? The last thing you and I need to do is talk negatively about ourselves.

Connect the Dots

Do you have trouble getting along with people? Understand that our relationships with God, ourselves, and other people are all interconnected. If we're not at peace with ourselves, we can't possibly be at peace with others (see 1 Peter 3:11). Many of us have strife inside ourselves, which causes us not to be at peace. Instead, we continually judge, analyze, and criticize ourselves and others.

I know this for a fact because I used to be such a hard person to get along with, yet I thought everyone else had a problem. I just wished they would stop making me mad! Then God showed me I can't give something away that I don't have myself. Also, I didn't like anyone else because deep down inside, I really didn't like myself. I couldn't get along with anyone else because I couldn't get along with myself.

If we concentrate on all we think is wrong with us, we'll feel insecure and depressed. If we look at all we think is right with us, we risk becoming proud and haughty. We need to look at Jesus because He's the Author and Finisher of our faith.

R-E-S-P-E-C-T Yourself

God wants us to feel right about ourselves and respect the fact that He started this work in us, and He's the only One who can finish it (see Philippians 1:6). We may not be spiritually, physically, or emotionally where we'd like to be, but the Bible tells us to keep pressing toward the mark of perfection until Jesus returns (see Philippians 3:14). This doesn't mean He won't correct us, but we know He is full of forgiveness and mercy, which we continually need in life. When we meet Jesus, whatever is wrong with us is going to instantly be fixed. Whatever needs to be finished will completely be finished at that point. So keep your eyes on the finish line and put your confidence in God alone (Philippians 3:3).

Judge Not

Hebrews 12:2 says, "[Look] away [from all that will distract] to Jesus, Who is the Leader and the Source of our faith." It tells us that when we take our eyes off of Jesus and look at everything that is wrong with us, it distracts us from Him, from the call of God on our lives, from prayer, and from fulfilling our destinies.

This doesn't mean that we shouldn't examine ourselves, but it's another thing to judge ourselves. *Examining* means we know our faults, and we take them to God and let Him change us. But *judging* means we pass a sentence on ourselves that we don't deserve to be blessed and God can't use us because we're too bad.

> God loves with an everlasting love. Even when we do dumb stuff, He sees our heart. He loves us just the way we are right now and who He is making us to be.

LORD,
teach me to laugh!

The ability to laugh is truly a gift from God—an expression of a joy-full heart. Unfortunately, laughter for most people is based on circumstances. But as believers, we can laugh even when everything goes wrong, because Jesus is our joy. He is the Vine, and we are the branches. As we learn to abide in Him, we will produce the fruit of His character, and one of those fruits is joy. In Christ, we can have overflowing joy, and when joy overflows, there is bound to be laughter (see John 15:1–11).

When God gives me an opportunity to laugh, I cut loose and get the most I can out of it because it seems to "air me out," refreshing me all over.

Laughter Starts From a Heart of JOY

When we accept Jesus Christ as our Lord and Savior, the fullness of God comes to live inside us (see Colossians 2:9–10). In other words, the Divine Seed that will produce all of the fruit of God's Spirit—including joy—is in us (see 1 John 3:9). It is not something we are trying to *get*—it is something we already *have*.

God wants the life of His Holy Spirit to flow freely in us and through us to touch others. But if we have allowed our soul to be clogged with resentment, bitterness, unforgiveness, worry, doubt, or depression, our spirit becomes greatly hindered. What we need to do is learn how to *release* it through laughter.

> "A happy heart is good medicine and a cheerful mind works healing."
>
> PROVERBS 17:22

Joy Is a Fruit of the SPIRIT

According to Galatians 5:22, *joy* is a fruit of the Spirit—not sadness, discouragement, or depression. If you and I will remain filled with the Holy Spirit throughout each day, He will inspire and energize us to be joy-full, in spite of outward circumstances. "In [God's] presence is *fullness* of joy" (Psalm 16:11). The presence of joy gives us the endurance to rise above our negative circumstances and enjoy all that God has for us.

One major way to stay full of the Spirit is to keep the *Word of God* in our mouth and in our mind, not *problems* (Joshua 1:8). Our excessive thoughts about a situation often lead to words that stir up negative emotions. If there is a purpose in talking about it, do so. Otherwise, commit the situation to God and fill your mind and your mouth with scriptures that reassure you that He is able to take care of it.

Another way to stay full of joy is to purposely choose to keep a song of praise in your heart and on your lips. Isaiah 61:3 says God has given us a *garment of praise* for the spirit of heaviness. This joy-full "jacket" is ours, but we have to *choose* to put it on daily.

Laughter Is Like ANESTHESIA

There are many scriptures that talk about how God uses the Word to heal us and change us. Psalm 107:20 says God sends forth His Word and *heals* us and rescues us from the pit and destruction. Hebrews 4:12 says that God's Word is *operative* on us, cutting out the "spiritual diseases" that make us sick.

Over the years I've been amazed by how people laugh spontaneously throughout my messages, especially when my content wasn't funny. I came to understand that God uses laughter to help people handle the correction that the Word often brings. People tell me later: "I desperately needed to laugh like that" or "I feel as if something heavy has been lifted off of me." God can and will use laughter to bring deep healing to our soul if we will let Him.

We All Have Reason to Be JOYFUL

Perhaps you're thinking, *Well, I don't have anything to laugh about!* That may seem true. But if you and I can't enjoy our lives until we are "problem free," we will live in sadness and never know the joy Jesus intended for us. Salvation alone is reason enough to be exceedingly joyful. Here's the truth: my worst day with the Lord is far better than my best day without Him.

Victory is not in the absence of problems; it is in the presence of God's power, which is greater than any adverse circumstances. Draw close to God and make the choice to rejoice. Learn to laugh in and through the difficulties of life. Pray and ask God to teach you to laugh more, and ask Him to show you things to laugh about. When the devil launches an attack against you, retaliate with joy and laughter, with singing and praise to God. If God can help me learn to laugh—a choleric woman who was sober faced for many years—I know He can help you!

"He who has a glad heart has a continual feast [regardless of circumstances]."

PROVERBS 15:15

JOYCE MEYER
#1 *NEW YORK TIMES* BESTSELLING AUTHOR

100
ways to
Simplify
your Life

EXCERPTS FROM
JOYCE MEYER'S
UPCOMING BOOK

EVERYONE HAS THEM: those days where nothing seems to get done, except maybe what you've added to your already lengthy to-do list. Are you tired most of the time? Are you spent? Do you find yourself wishing for a better day—a simpler day? Too many things compete for your limited resources of attention, energy, and time. You may be suffocating and not even know it. If you feel like this, you're not alone.

100 Ways

Most people today live complicated lives that leave them frustrated and confused, weary and worn out. But I have good news: your life does not have to be that way. You can choose a life of simplicity, fruitfulness, fulfillment, peace, and joy. I want to warn you, however, unless you are determined not to, you will do what everyone else does. You will get sucked up in the system and spend your life wishing things were different, never realizing you are, in fact, the only one who can change things. Unless we are resolute and remain undaunted in our quest for simplicity, we are destined for complication and frustration.

I recall a time when I was complaining to God about my schedule being absolutely insane. How could anyone be expected to do all I had in front of me? Then the realization hit me that I was the one who made my schedule and nobody could change it but me. You can spend your life wishing things were different, but wishing won't change anything. Smart decision making and decisive action is what changes things. If you picked up this book looking for change, are you willing to make a decision and follow it up with action?

I wasted many years hoping life would change and things would calm down until I finally realized life itself doesn't change; in fact, it has the potential to get worse. I understood my only real option was to change my approach to life. I had to say no to another day of rushing around and feeling frustrated. I didn't want the doctor giving me another prescription to mask another symptom of the real problem—stress.

In my search for simplicity, I have come to believe life can never be simple unless I learn to approach all things simply. It is my attitude toward each event in life that determines how easy or complex each situation will be. Perhaps life is complicated because people are complicated. Is it possible that life is not complicated, but rather, individuals complicate life in the way they approach it?

I discovered it wasn't really life or circumstances or other people as much as it was me that needed to change. My problem wasn't the problem—I was the problem! When you spend your life in frustration trying to change the world and everyone in it, you fail to realize it could be you just need to change your approach to life. It can be very easy for someone to live an entire lifetime and never entertain the notion that the way they do things is the real problem.

Increase Your Joy

Have you ever attempted to have friends over for what you initially intended to be a simple afternoon of food, fellowship, and fun, but somehow, it turned into a complicated nightmare? I remember those days vividly. I'd be at church on Sunday and, without much forethought, invite three couples over for the following Sunday to a barbecue. My initial thought was hot dogs and hamburgers on the grill, baked beans, potato chips, and iced tea. My motive was fellowship and fun, but by the time the guests arrived, I didn't even want them there. Fun was not going to happen, at least not for me. Why? I turned my simple get-together into a nightmare of preparation, expensive food, and fourteen people instead of the original six. My complicated approach to life and my complicated thought process convinced me hot dogs and hamburgers weren't nice enough so I bought steaks we could not afford. My potato chips turned into a huge bowl of homemade potato salad. The simple baked beans became four side dishes I labored over.

Insecure and wanting to impress everyone, I had to spend the week cleaning and getting everything in the house to the point where I thought it would be impressive. Of course, the lawn chairs were old, so I bought new ones. I got angry at Dave because I thought he wasn't helping me enough, and by the time our friends arrived, I resented them, wished they hadn't come, and had a miserable day of pretending to be the happy hostess when in reality I was frustrated and miserable.

I could not figure out why I wasn't able to enjoy much of anything in life until God revealed to me I was killing my joy with complication. For years, I prayed God would change the people and circumstances around me when, in reality, He wanted to change me and my approach to life. He wanted me to simplify so, ultimately, He could be glorified.

Let me share with you 100 ways to approach living that can simplify your life and, in turn, release and increase your joy. I believe they will dramatically improve the quality of your everyday experience if you incorporate them into the way you do things. Jesus said He came so we might have and enjoy our life in abundance (see John 10:10). His principles are simple. Faith is simple! Trusting God is simple! A childlike approach to Him is simple! The plan of salvation is simple!

Jesus offers us a "new way of living," and I believe it is a simple, yet powerful way that enables us to enjoy everyday life. Are you ready to simplify your life? Are you ready to say good-bye to the complexities you've allowed to take over? Let's get started.

Focus

Do One Thing at a Time

{ "The feeling of being hurried is not usually the result of living a full life and having no time. It is, on the contrary, born of a vague fear that we are wasting our life. When we do not do the one thing we ought to do, we have no time for anything else—we are the busiest people in the world."

ERIC HOFFER

Looking away [from all that will distract] to Jesus, Who is the Leader and the Source of our faith [giving the first incentive for our belief] and is also its Finisher [bringing it to maturity and perfection].

HEBREWS 12:2 }

When we do things without truly focusing our minds on them, we immediately decrease our strength to do the work before us and do it well. By putting our hands to one thing and our mind to another, we divide the muscle behind our abilities and we make the task much more difficult. It's like removing an egg yolk from the egg white—both can be used separately but the result isn't as effective (or tasty) as it would be if we leave the egg whole. However, by directing all of our faculties to the one thing we are doing on a particular day, at that hour, at that moment, we find it much easier to do. The ability to concentrate and stay focused can only come from discipline.

The apostle Paul tells us in Philippians 4:6 to be anxious for nothing. Anxious people are always trying to live ahead of where they currently are. They spend today trying to figure out tomorrow and the result is the loss of simplicity. God expects us to trust Him with tomorrow just as He instructed the Israelites to do when they crossed the barren wilderness, pressing toward the Promised Land.

Practice living one day at a time; give yourself—your thoughts, your conversation, your energies, every part of you—to the day at hand.

Develop an ability to give yourself to what you are doing. You will sense an awareness enabling you to enjoy the current activity, instead of going through each day in a blur of activity and confusing thoughts which leave you drained and exhausted.

Do you fear you will not accomplish as much if you try to live this way? It's true you may not do as much, but you will also enjoy what you do a whole lot more. One key to simplicity is realizing that quality is far superior to quantity.

Enjoy

Be Satisfied with What You Have

"Contentment is not the fulfillment of what you want, but the realization of how much you already have."

ANONYMOUS

Let your character or moral disposition be free from love of money [including greed, avarice, lust, and craving for earthly possessions] and be satisfied with your present [circumstances and with what you have]; for He [God] Himself has said, I will not in any way fail you.

HEBREWS 13:5

The affluence of our Western culture has created an epidemic of coveting what everyone else has. People crave more and more, yet they don't enjoy what they already possess. A simple person is a satisfied person; they don't crave more of anything, but they do thoroughly enjoy what they have. They trust that more will come in due time.

Does "more" have the ability to make us happy as the world wants us to believe? The answer is No! In fact, the more we have, the more work we must do to take care of it. We may think "more" makes life easier, but in reality, it often complicates the day-to-day. The tenth commandment tells us not to covet; we aren't to want what others have. Paul states in Philippians 4:11 that he learned how to be content no matter what his circumstances were. Even hearing that statement reminds me of simplicity and ministers comfort to me.

There's nothing wrong with having things, but it is wrong to lust after them. When we feel we cannot be happy without something, we are lusting after it. We should develop the habit of asking God for what we want, and believe He will give it to us if, and when, it is right. This simple approach to life sets us free to enjoy life. Life is the journey, not the destination. Those who want to enjoy life must learn to enjoy the journey, which is filled with waiting. Eventually, we reach our destination only to begin again on a new journey to another place; therefore, to never enjoy the journey is to never enjoy life. Make a decision to begin thoroughly enjoying what you have. Thank God for it and be content.

Change

Regularly Reevaluate Commitments

{ "If you don't like something, change it; if you can't change it, change the way you think about it."

MARY ENGELBREIT

Come to Me, all you who labor and are heavy-laden and overburdened, and I will cause you to rest. [I will ease and relieve and refresh your souls.]

MATTHEW 11:28 }

Jesus says He wants to give us rest. He invites us to come and, perhaps, He wants to give us an opportunity to reevaluate our commitments. He wants us to find what isn't necessary and get rid of it. Anytime we feel like life has lost the simple flow it should have and, instead, has become burdensome and heavy, we should take those weights to Jesus. Life was not meant to make us feel dragged down and weary. We are not mules who spend their lives carrying a burden. We are God's children with a blood-bought right to peace and joy.

Things in life are always changing and shifting. In order to grow, we must change also, and our commitments must change to match the changes happening in our lives. My youngest daughter, Sandra, worked on our ministry staff for fifteen years. She traveled with me, was in charge of our helps ministry, and did many things she enjoyed. When she felt ready to have children, she also thought she could still work, at least part-time. Much to her surprise, she had twins and it wasn't long before she was in tears because her life was so complicated. She knew she had to make the difficult decision to not work for several years. The decision made a big difference in their family finances, and she didn't want to feel left out of things at the ministry. I respect her so much because she valued a peaceful, simple lifestyle more than money and position, and I believe God is blessing her in special ways because of her difficult decision.

I believe we often forfeit many blessings God has stored up for us because we are not willing to reevaluate commitments and cut out things that God is finished with or are no longer bearing fruit. Just because you have always done something does not mean you should always do it. We

Let Go

can easily get into a rut and find ourselves feeling bored and bland for no reason other than we have done too much of the same thing for too long and we need a change.

It is easy to cut things off you don't want to do, but what about when God asks you to lay something down your emotions are not ready to give up? What if it is something you have helped birth and build and feel attached to and even responsible for? Would you be willing to let go of something you still enjoy, in obedience to God, in order to simplify your life? Obedience is not always easy. Much of the time it involves sacrificing our ways for God's way. Sometimes we don't understand why, but those are the times when we need to trust Him and keep moving forward. God never asks us to do anything that won't eventually make our lives better.

Don't be afraid to regularly reevaluate and make changes you need to make in order to keep your life on the simple track.

Start Fresh

It Is Never Too Late to Begin Again

"How wonderful it is that nobody need wait a single moment before starting to improve the world."

ANNE FRANK

It is because of the Lord's mercy and loving-kindness that we are not consumed, because His [tender] compassions fail not. They are new every morning; great and abundant is Your stability and faithfulness.

LAMENTATIONS 3:22–23

Hopelessness is a burden none of us needs to endure because, with God, it is never too late to begin again. He is the God of new beginnings. Jonah went in the opposite direction of the one God instructed, but God let him have a fresh start once he admitted his mistake.

It is never too late to pray and ask for God's help and forgiveness. The devil wants us to feel hopeless. He loves words like "never" and "the end." He says, "This is the end of everything. You have messed up and can never overcome your bad choices." We must remember to look to God's Word for truth, because the devil is a liar.

The Bible is filled with stories about people who experienced new beginnings. Receiving Jesus as our Savior is the ultimate new beginning. We become new creatures with an opportunity to learn a new way of living. The Bible even says in Ephesians 4:23 that we must be constantly renewed in our minds and attitudes. If you ever thought or displayed an attitude thinking it was too late for you to have a good life, good relationships, or hope for the future, then you need to renew your mind right away. Choose to think according to God's Word and not how you feel. Nobody is a failure unless they choose to stop trying. Life gets a lot sweeter and easier if we live with the attitude that says, "I will do my best today and I trust God will do the rest. Tomorrow I will begin again and I will never quit or give up."

thoughts " We only get one chance at life. It is not something we can redo, so we should make sure the first 'go around' is great. It is not God's will that we merely exist and try to make it through each day. He wants us to live joyfully and expectantly, to experience true happiness.

To *be your best*, love and enjoy today, make the most of every moment, and look forward with passion and confidence to the great future God has in store for you as you embrace your tomorrows. Hopefully your newfound happiness will rub off on all the people around you—and eventually the entire world will be a better place! "